QUICK OVERVIEW OF GOOGLE DRIVE AND FILE HANDLING

This book concerns itself with Google Sheets, not the entire Google Drive system. If you want to know more about file handling, and other Chromebook-specific procedures, then check out the first book in this series, Going Chromebook: Living Life in the Cloud. Still, in order to use Sheets, you need to be able to get to your files, so let's do a quick refresher. You start out by pointing your web browser at

`http://drive.google.com`

Log in if necessary, and you'll see something like the following:

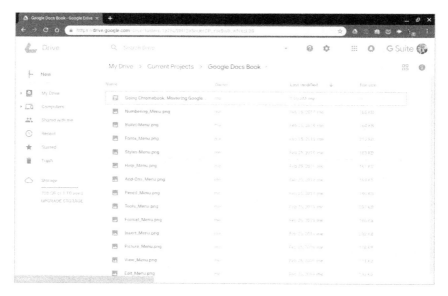

File View on Google Drive

In the left pane, you see a button for "New" and options to view "My Drive," "Computers," "Shared with Me," and a few other locations. You can click on the little arrow next to "My Drive" to navigate through various folders in your Google Drive.

At the top of the screen, there is a box to search through all your documents, and a line that tells you where you are inside of your drive. In the screenshot, I am in the folder "My Drive > Current Projects > Google Docs Book," and it lists the files in that folder. If you're new to all this, you won't see any files.

In the top-right section, you'll see the G Suite (or Google Docs) logo and an icon. You can click on this icon to access your Google Account. To the left of that is a bell for notifications, a grid icon that lets you quickly access other Google Apps, a gear icon for settings, and a question mark for the help screens.

If you right-click on a file, you'll see a screen like the following:

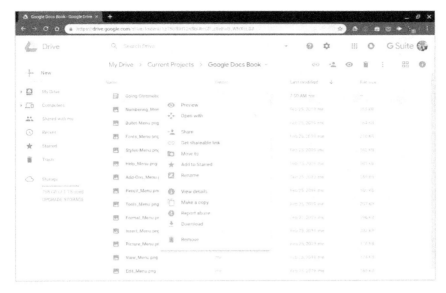

Right Click on a File for the Context menu

By right-clicking on a file, you can perform various actions on that file. The most common actions are moving files, renaming files, and removing (deleting) files, and these are all done here. You can also move files around by dragging them (click and hold the mouse button and then move the cursor while holding down the button) to other folders and locations.

To open a file, you simply double-click it. Alternately, you can choose "Open with..." from the menu above.

To create a new file, click on the "New" button on the left, which pops up a menu:

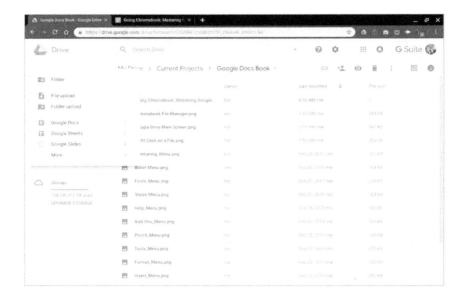

New File

Here, you can create a new folder, upload a file or folder from your computer, or create a new Google Doc (word processing document), Sheet (spreadsheet), or Slides (presentations).

Note on File Types: Google stores most files unchanged on their servers. Office files (Microsoft Word, Excel, and PowerPoint) can be stored unchanged if you wish, but in order to edit them with Google Docs, they need to be converted to Google's own format, **which only exists in the cloud**. You cannot download Docs, Sheets, or Slides formatted documents– in order to download these files to your computer, they need to be converted to Microsoft Office formatted files.

If you choose "File upload" or "Folder upload" from the menu above, you will have the option to either upload your Microsoft Word, Excel, and PowerPoint files unchanged or convert them to Google Documents format. Non-Office files just upload to Google Drive without alteration. If you change Office-formatted files to Google's format, you can edit the resulting files in Google Docs, Slides, or

Sheets. These **cloud-only file types** need to be re-converted to Word, Excel, and PowerPoint if you need to download them again.

Although Sheets is very good at this conversion process, in the case of very complicated files, sometimes things go wrong, so keep a backup of your original Microsoft documents until you have verified that everything converts properly. If you don't need to edit the files, there's no reason to convert them to Docs files– you can store literally any kind of file in Google Drive.

Part One

GOOGLE SHEETS COMMANDS AND MENUS

THE TOP SECTION OF THE GOOGLE SHEETS INTERFACE

To create a Sheet from scratch, from the main Google Drive screen, click on the big button that says "+ NEW" in the top-left of your browser window. Next, click on "Google Sheets," and you'll get a new, blank, document similar to the screenshot below. Once you've created a new spreadsheet, it's time to do something with it. In this chapter, we'll look at all the possibilities, features, and options that are contained within the many menus in Google Sheets.

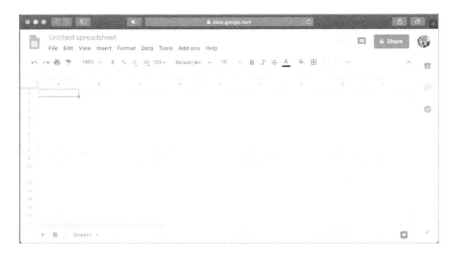

A Blank Google Sheets Document

At the very top of the screen, you see the Chrome browser URL and toolbar. In the screenshot, it's the dark bar at the top, and if you are using some other browser than Chrome (like Firefox or Safari for example), yours will look slightly different, but similar in all the important ways.

There are four major parts of the interface, and we'll cover them as they move from the top to the bottom of the screen. We'll look at the "Special Icons" (Filename, comments, sharing) first. Then we'll look at the menus (File, Edit, View, etc.). Third is the toolbar, and last is the big document window.

Google makes it easy to type in your numbers and text, add pictures, tables, charts, and most other Images that you'd like included in a spreadsheet.

SPECIAL ICONS

Beneath the Chrome Browser controls is the actual Google Sheets screen. The green icon in the upper far-left corner of the window indicates that this is a Sheets document (Docs are blue, Sheets are green, Slides are yellow).

Next to that is the filename, in the screen above, it's the very-generic default name: "Untitled Document." To name your file, just click on the "Untitled Document" text and start typing; when you hit 'Enter' after typing the name, the document will start saving with that filename. In the screen-shot below, I have renamed the spreadsheet to be "Brian's Spreadsheet."

Next to the filename are the "Starred" and "Move to..." icons. These aren't in the screenshot above because that file has not been named or saved yet. Once you give the file a name, these two icons will appear right next to the file name. Marking a file as "Starred" is like making it a favorite in some other systems- from the main Google Drive screen, you can click on a menu to show your starred files. It's just a way to get faster access to your most-often-used files. The "Move to..." icon does what it sounds like: it allows you to move the file to a different folder within your Google Drive. You can see these in the partial screenshot below.

Top Section of Document Screen

Also, once you've given your document a name, you should start to see "All changes saved in Drive" appear from time to time, occasionally alternating with "Saving..." You never need to explicitly save your work in Google Sheets, as it does that automatically and regularly.

Over toward the right side is a bent arrow icon. This is the *Activity Dashboard*. If you aren't going to collaborate with other writers, you won't use this. If you are collaborating, this allows you to see which of your collaborators have looked at your document.

Next to the Activity Dashboard icon is the *Comment History* icon, which looks like a comic-book speech bubble. Again, if you collaborate, here you can read what others have commented about this document. It's not completely useless for single-users, as you can make notes and comments on your own work if you like. As an example, I have the screenshot below, where I have highlighted a few words, added a comment, and then looked at the Comment History.

You add a comment by clicking to highlight a cell, then right-clicking the mouse (or using a two-fingered trackpad click) to bring up a context menu, and choosing "Comment" from the list. All comments appear in little bubbles that appear when the cell is highlighted. Cells with comments have a little orange triangular mark in the cell's upper right-hand corner so you can see them quickly. The Comment History button is there to allow you to reply to other people's comments.

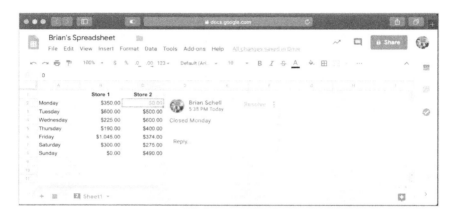

Adding a Comment

OK, so back to the top bar. There's a big green "Share" button. If you click it, you'll get a pop-up dialog that looks like this:

Share with Others Dialog

You can add someone else's email address in the box to allow them access to the document. If you want to collaborate with someone, this is how you set that up. They'll be sent an email with an invitation to work on this document. By default, these people can read **and edit** your document. If you just want someone else to only be able to read your document without being able to change it, click on the "Get shareable link" button and copy the URL that it creates. Anyone who clicks on that URL can view the document in read-only mode. The "Advanced" option down at the bottom allows some additional options for more complex sharing.

The very top-right icon is to access your Google Account. You can sign out, personalize your icon, and other account-related things here.

And that's it for the "special icons."

THE MENUS

This is going to be the largest section of the book, as the majority of the functions and features are controlled here.

THE FILE MENU

The **File menu** (and all the other major menus) are located directly under the filename of the document.

The first thing you may notice is that there's no "Save" or "Save As…" choices. You've already named your file, so "Save As…" isn't needed. There is an option to "Make a copy…" which is the other main thing "Save As…" is often used for.

Also, the sheet is saved automatically every few seconds, so there's no need for a special "Save" choice.

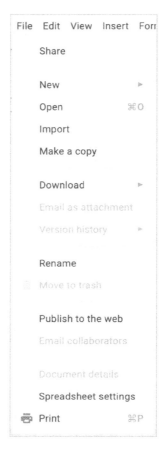

The File Menu

Share... This brings up the same Share menu that we discussed in the previous section.

New Allows you to create a new file. You have the option to make a Document, Spreadsheet, Presentation, Form, Drawing, or load something from a template. Most of these choices just create a new document using one of the Google Apps. **Template** brings up a large selection of pre-made documents for you to modify. Take a look at the various templates that are available when you get a few spare minutes- Not only can they save you a load of time by not forcing you to reinvent the wheel, many of them have powerful features that you can examine and possibly learn something new.

Template Gallery

Open... Brings up a file chooser and lets you open another document in a separate browser tab.

Make a copy... Lets you make a duplicate of the current file.

Download As I mentioned earlier, you cannot download a Google Sheet in its native cloud-based format, but you can download it in many other formats. Here you have a choice of Microsoft Excel (.xlsx), OpenDocument (.ods), Portable Document Format (.pdf), Comma-Separated values (.csv), Tab-separated values (.tsv), or as a zipped HTML Page. Lots of good choices!

Email as attachment... This brings up a window that allows you to enter an email address. The document, along with a note, will be emailed from your Gmail account to whomever you want.

Version History Shows changes and editing sessions made each day. You can revert to previous sessions, and even name sessions, like "Made big changes to Sheet_3!" for example. So, if you add a bunch of stuff today and find out tomorrow that it's all wrong, you can revert back to yesterday's version without too much trouble.

Version History

Rename... This highlights the file name at the top of the screen, allowing you to rename the file. You can also just click and change the file name directly by clicking on it.

Move Allows you to move the file from its current location to another folder in your Google Drive.

Move to Trash Sends your spreadsheet to Google Drive's trash can. You can retrieve documents or delete them permanently from the main Google Drive screen. Note that just like on a desktop computer, removing a file doesn't immediately delete it. It just moves it to the trash can, where you can restore it later if the need arises.

Publish to the web... Offers two main options. **Linking** gives you a link you can share with anyone. If they click on the link, they can see your sheet. **Embedding** allows you to include the sheet within another web page.

Email collaborators... Lets you send a message to a specific collaborator, or to everyone who is collaborating on this document. This is simpler than just using Gmail, since Sheets already knows the emails of all the invited collaborators.

Document details... Tells the folder location, file owner, the creation date, and last edited date for the document.

Spreadsheet Settings Lets you change the locale of the document. This affects things like date formatting, currency symbols, etc. You can also change the language that the Google Sheets menus appear in as well as set your time zone. In the "Calculation" tab, you can set how formulas with circular references are calculated and how certain time and random number generators behave.

Print... Brings up the print dialog box. You can set the Destination (an actual printer or the ability to save as a PDF file), which pages you want to print, how many pages you want to print on each sheet of paper, whether or not to include headers, footers, page numbers, date, time, and other options.

Note that a Chromebook will only work with **Google Cloud Print** compatible printers– you cannot just plug in a wired printer. If you are running Chrome on a non-Chromebook computer, then you should be able to print to any printer, just as you would with any other app.

Printing Options Dialog

THE EDIT MENU

Next up is the Edit menu. Mostly, these options are the same as those available in word processors or other spreadsheet systems, so if you already know how to cut and paste, there's not much new here.

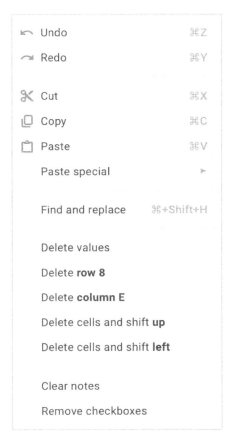

Edit Menu

Undo Undo can go back and restore the last thing you changed. There are hundreds of levels of undo, so if you've heavily edited a sheet, you can go "back in time" quite a long way.

Redo If you hit the undo feature too many times, you can start moving forward, redoing changes that have recently been undone.

Cut Select some text and "cut" it. Cutting visually deletes the selected text from your document but saves it in the clipboard, an unseen, temporary holding buffer that contains items that have been **Cut** or **Copied**. If you move your cursor to another point in the document and click on **Paste**, the cut text will be pasted in at the cursor's location. This is the easiest way to move a block of text from one location in your document to another.

Copy This does exactly the same thing as **Cut**, but it does not delete the original text. When you hit **Paste**, you will insert an identical copy of what had been copied.

Paste Inserts whatever is in the clipboard. You can cut and paste text, images, drawings, charts, tables, formulas, and most other objects. You can also paste more than one copy of whatever is in the clipboard, making it an easy way to repeat text.

Paste special This is the same as Paste, can be limited to pasting

- Cell values Only
- Cell formatting Only
- Everything except borders
- Copy only the column widths
- Formulas only
- Data Validation rules only
- Conditional Formatting only
- Transposed (vertical lists become horizontal and vice-versa)

Find and Replace Brings up the dialog box shown below. If you want to search for a specific word or phrase, enter it in the "Find" box and click "Next." If you want to find it again, click the "Next" button as many times as you want to cycle through occurrences of the word in your document. If you want to find a word and replace it with another word, then put the new word in the "Replace with" box. In the screenshot, I am replacing the word "This" with the word "That."

Find and replace ✕

Find   123

Replace with   222|

Search   All sheets ▾

☐ Match case

☐ Match entire cell contents

☐ Search using regular expressions Help

☐ Also search within formulas

Find   Replace   Replace all   **Done**

Find and Replace

There are a few additional options for Find and Replace. You can choose to only find words that match the same capitalization: "This" but not "this" would be found. There is also an option for using "regular expressions," an advanced way of describing text that you want to look for. Regular expressions are very complicated, but extremely powerful if you learn how they work (there are entire books devoted to regular expressions). Lastly, you can choose to search for the text within formulas instead of limiting the search to text and numbers only.

Also, it's not in the menu, but if you press **ctrl-f** (The **ctrl** key and the letter "**f**"), a small search bar opens near the top of the screen that allows you to quickly search for a word or value.

Delete values Deletes the highlighted text. It does not delete formatting in the cell(s).

Delete row/Delete column Allows you to delete the entire selected row or columns

Delete cells and shift up/down Allows you to delete the selected cells, not necessarily the entire row. Depending on the positioning of the cell, other cells may shift to replace the deleted data.

Clear Notes If the selected cells contain a note, it will be deleted. This is good for when a spreadsheet you have finished creating is "ready for production," and you want to get rid of any hard-to-find notes that you may have forgotten somewhere.

Remove Checkboxes Checkboxes are great for to-do lists and other things. Clicking on them checks or unchecks them, but this menu option deletes the checkboxes in the selection completely.

SELECTING TEXT

There are a number of different ways to select text within Sheets:

1. Position the cursor at the place where you want to start selecting text.
2. You can click the mouse button and hold it down as you move the mouse, and release the mouse when you done selecting text.
3. Alternately, position the cursor at the place where you want to start selecting text and hold down the SHIFT key and the arrow keys to select text.
4. If you have a touch screen, you can double-click on a cell to select it and then use the "drag handles" to expand your selection, similar to selecting text on a phone.

USING THE KEYBOARD

This is as good a time as any to talk about *keyboard shortcuts*. If you look at any of the menus, you will see the options discussed above, but next to many of them are keyboard shortcuts. For example,

ctrl-z is for Undo
ctrl-y is for Redo
ctrl-x is for Cut
ctrl-c is for Copy
ctrl-v is for Paste
ctrl-a is for Select all

and so forth.

Not all editing functions have control keys, but many do. In the beginning, you should probably just use the mouse as you learn what Google Sheets can do, but as you get more comfortable with the system, learning these keyboard shortcuts can save you a considerable amount of time. The ones I mentioned in the preceding paragraph are some of the most helpful ones.

You can find the current list of all keyboard shortcuts here:

`https://support.google.com/`
`chromebook/answer/183101`

Again, not many people learn all of these, but look through the list and pick a few to get started. This list is included in its entirety later in the book.

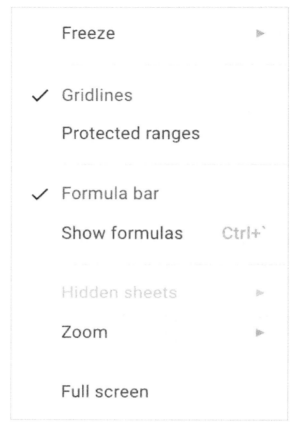

The View Menu

THE VIEW MENU

Freeze Freezing columns or rows is nice when you have column or row headings that you want to keep *always visible* on the screen, even when the user scrolls through the sheet. For example, if you freeze row 1, then no matter how many hundreds of lines down you delve into the spreadsheet, row 1 is still visible at the top of the document window. This submenu gives you the choice of freezing 1 or 2 rows or columns, or everything up to the currently selected cell. Another option is to freeze "none," which unfreezes whatever you already had frozen.

Gridline turns off or on the "Grid" that covers the main document window. The cells are still there, but the "graph paper" look goes away. This does not affect borders that you create yourself.

Protected Ranges If you set a range of cells to be protected, or non-editable by certain users, the users will see the cells have a checkered background color. This checkering can be turned off here. The cells are still locked & protected, they just don't stand out with a weird background anymore.

Formula bar Makes the Formula Bar just below the top toolbar become invisible.

Show Formulas Normally, you don't want the user to see the formulas used to compute values, but sometimes when you are creating a spreadsheet, you need to see where all the formulas are. This turns on that view, as in the example below:

Spreadsheet with "Display Formulas" on (See row 9)

Hidden Sheet It's a lot like the Protected Cells feature above. You have the option to hide entire sheets from the user. If you want to be able to see sheets that have already been hidden, click this option.

Zoom Lets you select from various common preset levels of zoom if you want to fit more or fewer cells on the screen at once or just to make everything bigger.

Full Screen This hides all the menus and toolbars and fills the browser window with your document. Hit the **ESC** key to return your screen to normal, windowed mode. *HINT*: just using Google Sheets' full screen mode still leaves all the Chrome browser URL bar and toolbars visible. To go to *true* full-screen mode, also click on the Chrome Browser's "Customize" button (also known as the "Three-Dots Menu," and choose the full-screen mode for Chrome. You'll see nothing on your screen but your document. If you aren't using the Chrome browser, look around; most other browsers have a similar feature.

The Icon for Full-Screen Mode is to the right of the 100% in the center

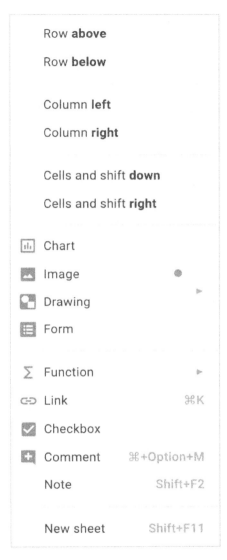

The Insert Menu

INSERT MENU

The Insert menu is where you Insert various non-text elements into your documents. There are many submenus and options here, so this is one of the more complex sections of Sheets:

Row above/below Inserts a new, blank row above (or below) of the currently selected cell.

Column left/right Inserts a new, blank column to the left (or right) of the currently selected cell.

Cells and shift down/right This one will insert one or more blank cells and shift the contents beneath that cell downward (or to the right if choosing the other option).

Chart inserts a new, not-yet-configured chart. You start off with a screen that looks something like this:

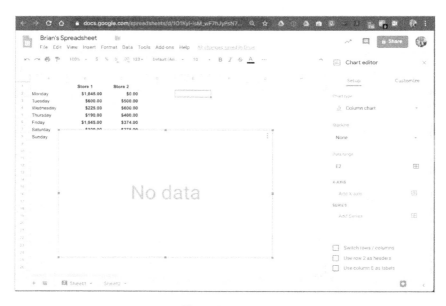

Chart editor Screen

To make your chart, you'll need to fix some settings in the Chart editor in the right-hand pane.

The first thing you need to decide is the chart type. There are variations of pie chart, line chart, and most of the common styles:

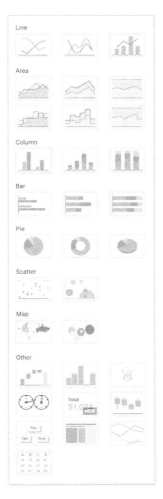

Chart Types

With the sample data in my example spreadsheet, I want to create an Area Chart. I click on the icon of the type of chart I want to make.

Next, there are some stacking options. In an Area Chart, these determine whether or not your data stacks on top of each other or overlays each other. I want them to overlay, so I choose "None" for stacking.

Next is the tricky one, Data Range. This is how you tell Google

Sheets which numbers to use in the chart. You start by entering a range of cells for the first range. In this case, B2 through B8, so I can either type B2:B8 or use the mouse to select that range on the spreadsheet. Since I want to compare Store 1 and Store 2, I want to "Add another range," where I type or mouse-select the range C2 through C8.

Select a data range

B2:B8   🗑

C2:C8   🗑

Add another range

Cancel   OK

Select Data Range

You can add as many ranges as you want, but in this example, I only need two, so I click "OK" at this stage.

Now, we can see that we have a workable, but pretty basic-looking chart. It's got the numbers on the Y-axis, but nothing on the bottom X-axis. If we click the button marked "Add X-axis" we can select the days of the week from the spreadsheet or enter the range A2:A8.

This might be all you need. At this point, you can go back and change the "Chart type" to other variations and see if there's something you like better. All the ranges and axes will remain as they are, but the shape of the graph can change in dozens of different ways. Try it as a line chart or a column chart— they both look good. Now, for this example, I'm going to switch to "Column Chart" because it's easy, and I think maybe it looks better.

In order to customize the chart even more, the chart editor has two tabs. We just worked through the "Setup" tab. The "Customize" tab has a bunch more options.

Working down through the options in the "Customize" tab, I add the feature "3D" under the "Chart Style" options. Under "Chart and axis titles" option, I add "Store 1 vs. Store 2 Last Week" as Title Text, and also choose to make the color for this blue. Lastly, under "Series," I change the color to deep red for column 1 and bright red for column 2. There are other options that you can experiment with at any time, but Google Sheets generally picks decent defaults and attractive charts without needing too much fiddling around. Here's my final chart:

Completed Chart Example

Image You can insert most image formats into Google Sheets. The submenu for this menu item offers **Image in cell** and **Image over cells**:

- **Image in cell** The first option allows you to link or upload an image and place it inside a single cell, limiting the size of the image to however large that cell is.

- **Image over cells** The second option lets you import an image that "floats" wherever you decide to place it, possibly overlapping and "covering up" other cells.

You'll also notice that a selected image has little "handles" in the corners and the middle of each side. If you click on these and drag them around, you can resize the image. Dragging on the **side handles** stretches and squashes the image, sometimes distorting it. Dragging from the **corner handles** expands or reduces the entire image proportionally.

Drawing Google Drawings is a whole different Google app, free and included with your Google Drive account. It allows you to make vector graphics drawings, similarly to Adobe Illustrator, Affinity Designer, and other vector graphics apps. This app is worthy of a book unto itself someday, but for now, remember that you can either load in a complete drawing or begin a new drawing using this menu item:

Drawing Mode

If you are curious about the full-scale Google Drawing app, you can find more information here:

`https://docs.google.com/drawings`

We aren't going to get into all the options here, as the app is complex enough for its own book, but just keep in mind that you can easily draw any shape that you might want to include in your spreadsheet.

Form refers to **Google Forms**, another Google app that allows you to create interactive forms that anyone online can fill out. You can make an attractive form with fill-in-the-bank, multiple choice, single sentence, time and dates, yes-or-no, and lots of other response types. You can set the form to insert the submitted data into your spreadsheet, thereby creating a data acquisition app. This is a super-powerful feature, and we'll discuss it more fully later on in this book.

Function This is where all the math functionality of a spreadsheet comes into play.

Link Allows you to add some kind of hyperlink to your document. You can enter a text label, followed by the link itself, which can be an external web link, another sheet in this spreadsheet, or even a range of cells that you can jump to. Click on a cell and choose this menu item to insert a function in that cell. Different functions are categorized by what they do, as shown here:

SUM

AVERAGE

COUNT

MAX

MIN

All   ►

Array   ►

Database   ►

Date   ►

Engineering   ►

Filter   ►

Financial   ►

Google   ►

Info   ►

Logical   ►

Lookup   ►

Math   ►

Operator   ►

Parser   ►

Statistical   ►

Text   ►

Web   ►

Learn more

Various Function Categories

Each of these categories has a handful of functions you can use to do calculations, database lookups, logical comparisons, statistical computations, or whatever you need. There are hundreds of functions, most of which are way beyond my mathematical ability to explain. Still, if you click on "Learn more" at the bottom of the menu, a list with all the functions will load. It can also be found at:

https://support.google.com/docs/table/25273

Checkbox Inserts a checkbox into the current cell. This checkbox can be clicked on or off with the mouse. This can be paired with "Data validation," which we will describe later, to actually have some programmatic meaning.

Comment is used mostly for collaboration with others. If someone enters a comment on a cell, it appears with an orange triangle in the upper right-hand corner. These can be seen by clicking on the cell, or by click on the "Open comment history" button in the top right-hand corner of the browser window.

Note Allows you to make a notation in a cell. The cell will get a small black triangle in the upper-right corner to remind you that it has a note.

New Sheet This adds a new sheet to the file. If you look at the bottom of the document window, you will see "Sheet1" on a tab. If you add more sheets, you'll see "Sheet2," "Sheet3," and so forth appear. These sheets can be renamed, re-ordered, deleted, duplicated, or color-coded as you prefer.

THE FORMAT MENU

The Format menu contains a vast number of options that allow you to change the appearance of various screen objects.

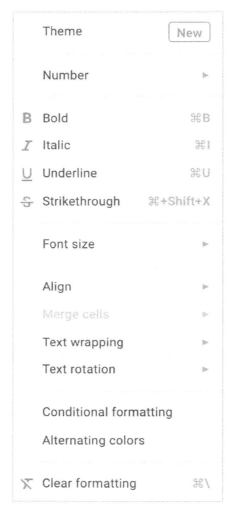

Format Menu

Many of the options in this list make a change to selected text. You can select text by dragging the mouse over a number of characters, words, or lines. You can also select text by holding down the SHIFT key and moving the cursor with the arrow keys.

Themes This allows you to change the appearance of selected cells. It will change the fonts and various colors of the cell contents.

You can click on the "Customize" button to see all the various things that the theme changes, and you can fine-tune them however you want:

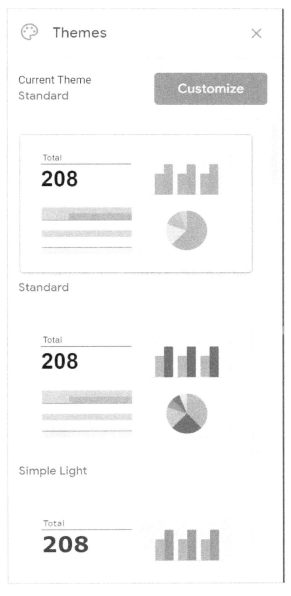

Themes Menu

Number brings up a submenu that allows you to describe what you want the numbers in the selected cell(s) to look like:

✓ Automatic	
Plain text	
Number	1,000.12
Percent	10.12%
Scientific	1.01E+03
Accounting	$ (1,000.12)
Financial	(1,000.12)
Currency	$1,000.12
Currency (rounded)	$1,000
Date	9/26/2008
Time	3:59:00 PM
Date time	9/26/2008 15:59:00
Duration	24:01:00
More Formats	▸

Number Menu

The various menu options will change the formatting of the number in the cell to look like the examples in the menu. At the bottom of the list is "More Formats," which gives access to additional dialogs where you can choose other forms of currency, other formats for dates, or even design your own customized number formats. Literally anything you need can be available through the "Custom" option.

Bold, Italic, Underline, Strikethrough Below the number menu, you have several options to change selected text. The next four menu options allow you to make text in selected cells **Bold**, *Italic*, Underlined, or Strikethrough.

Font Size You can choose the size of the font here. There are a dozen or so preset point sizes that you can choose from. If you need more precise control over font sizes, you can enter the point size you need in the font section of the toolbar, which we'll discuss later.

Align This gives you the option of making text within a cell line up on the left margin (left justified), or the right margin (right justified), or it can be centered on the line. In addition, you can also align text vertically, at the top, bottom, or middle of a cell.

Merge Cells You can use these functions to merge several individual cells into one big cell. This new, larger, cell can span multiple rows or multiple columns or both. Note that the function will be grayed out on the menu unless more than one cell is selected. There is also a function here to "ungroup" cells if you decide you want to try it differently.

Text Wrapping lets you control what to do with text that is too long to fit within a cell. There are three choices:

- *Overflow* allows the long text to flow across the following columns.
- *Wrap* makes the text wrap to the next line, which often makes the cell resize to make the cell "taller."
- *Clip* will cut off the text, leaving the cell's size alone, but showing only the portion of the text that will fit in the cell. The text is all really there; you just can't see it all.

Text Rotation Most text goes horizontally across the line of cells, but it doesn't have to be that way. With this menu option, you can make text slope at various angles or even have the text rotate to become vertical. As an alternate option, you can make the text stack vertically, making the line of text go up and down, but keeping the letters in their normal orientation.

Conditional Formatting is a powerful way to make certain parts of your data stand out. You can apply these conditions to a range of cells, and each cell in the range will be compared to some kind of condition that you set. If the cell qualifies, the contents will be displayed in the color of your choice. For example, if we want to highlight all the days where sales were greater than $400, we can do that. First, select a range of cells and then click on "Conditional Formatting." The appropriate pane will show up on the right-hand side of the screen like this:

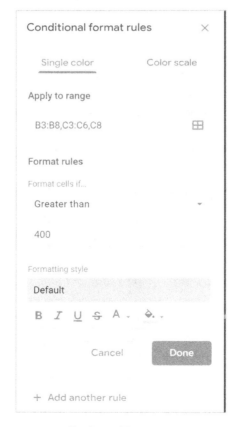

Conditional Formatting

From the dropdown menu "Format cells if..." there are many options, but in this case, we want to select "Greater than" and then type "400" in the value box. This will activate any cell greater than 400. You can then set the formatting style in the section just below that. I simply want to highlight these "good sales days" in red, so I choose the color red. This results in the following sheet:

	A	B	C
3	Tuesday	$600.00	$500.00
4	Wednesday	$225.00	$600.00
5	Thursday	$190.00	$400.00
6	Friday	$1,045.00	$374.00
7	Saturday	$300.00	$275.00
8	Sunday	$0.00	$490.00
9		$3,405.00	$2,639.00

Conditional Formatting Example

As you can see, the cells that contain values over $400 are shaded (my apologies if you're reading this book in a monochrome format and have to imagine the cells as red).

Alternating Colors if you select a range of cells and then use this tool, the background of every other line will change to a lightly shaded cell. The colors, details, and styles can be modified by using the settings pane on the right side of the screen. This can make long lists of data much easier to read and follow.

Alternating Colors Settings

Clear Formatting Removes any formatting in the selected cell(s) and sets all formatting options to the default.

DATA MENU

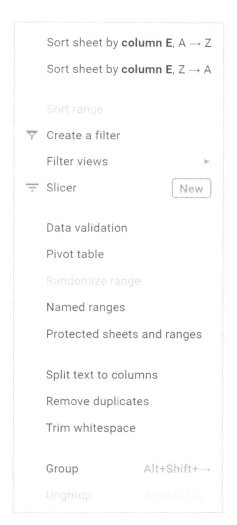

Data Menu

Sort Sheet by Column does exactly what it sounds like: it sorts the entire sheet, using the values in the selected column. The items in that column will be sorted from A to Z (or Z to A if you choose the second option), and all the lines of data in the spreadsheet will shift around as well. The entire *sheet* is sorted, based on the data in the selected column.

Sort Range sorts a selected range of cells. Unlike the previous option, *only* the selected cells are sorted; nothing happens to any other rows or columns.

Create a Filter allows you to *filter* what can be seen. It hides the cells that fulfill the conditions you set. A small inverted triangle of three lines will appear in the selected cell, such as what can be seen in the figure blow in cell B2:

	A	B	C
1		Store 1	Store 2
2	Monday	$1,045.00	$0.00
3	Tuesday	$600.00	$500.00
4	Wednesday	$225.	$600.00
5	Thursday		$400.00
6	Friday	$1,04	$374.00
7	Saturday	$300.00	$275.00
8	Sunday	$0.00	$490.00
9		$3,405.00	$2,639.00

The Filter Icon

By clicking on this icon, you can choose from various values, conditions, and sorting options that are smart: i.e. You can hide values over or under a certain amount, before or after a certain date, empty cells, or cells with some particular value. It lets you easily toggle these hidden values on or off. Filtering doesn't delete anything or change any values; all it does is "hide" rows or columns that meet the criteria that you set.

Slicers is a new feature that allows you to place a control anywhere on your spreadsheet that will allow the viewer to enter custom filters easily and much more obviously than the little filter triangles from the previous option.

You can set a slicer up so that it allows a user to filter in a column by setting up various conditions (greater than X, earlier than a date, and so forth), or they can be filtered by values:

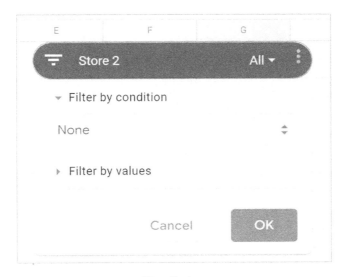

Slicer Options

Data Validation Allows you to create a drop-down list containing a list of values located elsewhere in the spreadsheet (or on a separate sheet).

The first step is to select the cell in which you want to place the drop-down box, then choose "Data Validation" from the Data menu:

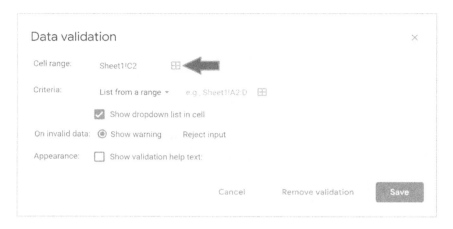

Data Validation Dialog

For example, let's say you want to create a drop-down list containing the days of the week.

The first field, "Cell range," allows you to put the drop-down list in multiple target cells. Most of the time, you'll put a drop-down list in a single cell, or you can just ignore this option if you've already selected the cell to contain the drop-down list.

Criteria: This is how you populate the list. You have numerous options here. The first option is "List from a Range." With this option, you could create a Sheet (or an area of the current sheet) that lists the seven possible answers, like this:

	A
1	Days of the week
2	Monday
3	Tuesday
4	Wednesday
5	Thursday
6	Friday
7	Saturday
8	Sunday

Days of the Week

Then you could enter the range A2:A8 to indicate the beginning and end of the list. You could also choose the "grid" symbol (per the arrow in the screenshot) to use the mouse to select the range.

Show dropdown list in cell does what it says: It allows you to see the possible values in the list. If you turn this off, you would need to type the value in the box, but only values on the list would be accepted.

On invalid data: can be set to either "Show warning" or "Reject input" depending on how serious the error is and how you want to handle that. In our "days of the week example," there are only seven legitimate answers, and anything else submitted in the box is not possible, so we would go with "Reject Input" if something else is entered here.

Appearance/Show Validation Help Text: You can type anything you want here, and if the user hovers the mouse over the dialog box, this text will appear as a tool tip. In our example, something like "Select the day of the week" might be a good choice.

Of course, there are only seven days in a week, and they never change, so using a range in the spreadsheet to enter those values is inefficient. In the dropdown box in "Criteria," we get the choice of entering:

- List from a Range
- List of Items
- Number
- Text
- Date
- Custom formula is
- Checkbox

We've already explained the first choice, "List from a range." The "List of items" would be the most efficient way to handle something like the days of the week. You could simply enter "Monday, Tuesday, Wednesday, Thursday, Friday, Saturday, Sunday" in the dialog, and Sheets will populate the dropdown list from that list.

Number, Text, and Date simply check to make sure that the data entered is the correct type. You cannot enter text information if the validation rule is set to "date" for example.

Custom formula will allow data to be entered if the value falls within the range allowed by the given formula. For example, if we want to make sure that only an odd number can be entered in cell C2 we can add the Data validation rule to cell C2, entering the formula =ISODD(C2), Then Sheets will only allow odd numbers to be entered. Most complex formulas can be entered this way.

Checkbox: Adds a checkbox to the cell, and the only possibility is that it's either checked or not.

Pivot Tables are a way to create detailed analyses of the data within one or more tables without actually altering the tables themselves. These can get very complex very quickly, and I've seen entire books devoted to the subject, so my example here will be somewhat brief.

I have a spreadsheet where I keep the "Horror Guys" movie reviews (it's a website and podcast that I co-host). I have the name of the movie in column A, then Kevin's (my co-host) rating of one through ten, and then in column C is my rating. Column D has a link to the text of the review on the website. It looks like this:

	Movie	Kevin	Brian	Text Review
1	Movie	Kevin	Brian	Text Review
2	13 Sins (2014)	8	8	http://www.horrorguys.com/13-sins-2014-review/
3	A Cure for Wellness (2018)	7	7	http://www.horrorguys.com/a-cure-for-wellness-2017-review/
4	Altered (2006)	10	6	http://www.horrorguys.com/they-will-find-you/
5	Birdbox (2018)	7	9	http://www.horrorguys.com/birdbox-2018-review/
6	Bride of Frankenstein (1935)	7	10	http://www.horrorguys.com/bride-of-frankenstein-1935-review/
7	Cabin in the Woods (2011)	10	10	http://www.horrorguys.com/cabin-in-the-woods-2011-review/
8	Cannibal Holocaust (1980)	3	3	http://www.horrorguys.com/cannibal-holocaust-1980-review/
9	Cemetery Man (1994)	8	8	http://www.horrorguys.com/cemetery-man-1994/
10	Coherence (2013)	6	7	https://www.horrorguys.com/coherence-2013-review/
11	Constantine: City of Demons (2018)	5	6	http://www.horrorguys.com/constantine-city-of-demons-2018-review
12	Contracted (2013)	6	8	http://www.horrorguys.com/contracted-2013-review/
13	Contracted: Phase 2 (2015)	6	5	http://www.horrorguys.com/contracted-phase-ii-2015-review/
14	Crucible of the Vampire (2019)	7	7	http://www.horrorguys.com/crucible-of-the-vampire-2019/
15	Darkness Falls (2003)	10	8	http://www.horrorguys.com/darkness-falls-2003-review/
16	Day of the Dead: Bloodlines (2018)	6	8	http://www.horrorguys.com/day-of-the-dead-bloodlines/
17	Death House (2017)	3	1	http://www.horrorguys.com/death-house-2017-review/
18	Don't Torture a Duckling (1972)	4	6	http://www.horrorguys.com/dont-torture-a-duckling-1972/
19	Dr. Phibes Rises Again (1972)	9	8	http://www.horrorguys.com/dr-phibes-rises-again-1972-review/
20	Dracula (1932)	8	8	http://www.horrorguys.com/dracula-1931-review/
21	Dracula's Daughter (1936)	7	6	http://www.horrorguys.com/draculas-daughter-1936-review/
22	Drag Me to Hell (2009)	6	8	http://www.horrorguys.com/drag-me-to-hell-2009-review/
23	Frankenstein (1931)	8	9	http://www.horrorguys.com/frankenstein-1931-review/

Movie Review Table

Now, suppose I want to see a list of the movies to which Kevin or Brian gave 10 stars. For this simple example, I *could* just use a filter to only show rows with a 10 rating, but pivot tables allow much more flexibility in what you can do. I *could* also sort the entire spreadsheet by column B (or C). That would work, but then that would *change* the layout of the main spreadsheet, which I want to be permanently alphabetical. I can't have it both ways.

Except that by using pivot tables, I can have it both ways. On the main spreadsheet, I can begin by selecting columns A through C. With those three columns highlighted, I would choose "Pivot table" from the "Data" menu. This brings up a dialog like this:

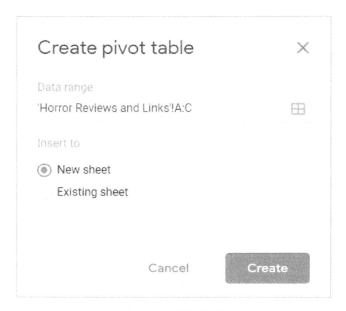

Create Pivot Table Dialog

The Data range listed is for the spreadsheet named "Horror Reviews and Links" and includes columns A through C. If it's not exactly what you want, you have the option of typing the range you want, or you can click on the little "select data range" icon next to the range listed. You also have the option of creating a new Sheet or adding it to an existing Sheet. I don't want to complicate my original data, so I'll put it on a new sheet, which I will name "Kevin's Reviews"

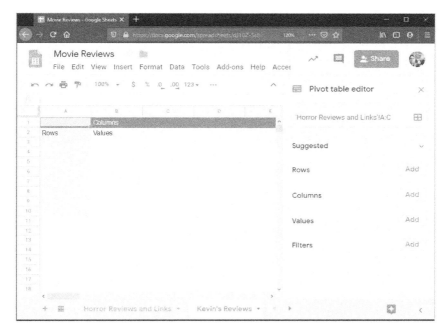

Main Pivot Table Creation Screen

Now it gets very flexible and potentially very complicated. In the pane on the right side of the screen, you have:

Suggested: If Google Sheets "understands" your table, it may suggest various data sets to include. In my example, it says "Sorry, there are no suggestions for this table." Google Sheets wasn't really programmed to understand movie reviews, which is no great surprise.

Rows, Columns, Values, and Filters: If you click on "Add" for any of these, the names of the three columns we selected (Movies, Kevin, Brian) show up in a list. Depending on which button you choose, the values in those columns will be imported into the new table as columns, rows, values, or filters. Under "Values" you also have the option to insert a Calculated field.

What I *want* to do is make a section of the table for Kevin's 10-star reviews, another for his 9-stars, and so on for all ten possible ratings.

If we choose "Rows" and add "Movies" and "Kevin" we'll simply see the list of movies and Kevin's reviews next to them, just like the original sheet. It's complicated, but fortunately, we can play around with this without any possibility of messing up our original data; this is one of the big benefits of Pivot Tables.

If I click on "Add" and choose "Kevin," I'll get the numbers one through ten in column A:

Added Kevin's Reviews to Column A of Pivot Table

Note that what's happened here is that Sheets has looked at the data and placed each unique rating on a line by itself. Since the ratings are all between one and ten, there are only ten possible values. I will click in the "Order" drop-down on the right side of the screen, and choose "Descending," since I am most interested in the higher numbers.

Next, I'll click on "Rows" and "Add" again, and this time pick "Movies." Suddenly, all the movies appear, sorted within the appropriate ratings. Here are the movies we saw in 2019 that Kevin rated ten out of ten. Below that are the ones that are 9 out of 10, and so on:

Pivot Table with Ratings and Movie Names

Let's say we're at the end of the year, and all I care about are the 10 out of 10 and 1 out of 10, So I can do something with *best and worst films of the year*. I can skip down to the "Filters" section, add a filter based on "Kevin" ratings, and then turn off everything except the ones and tens. This is all I want to do, so if I click somewhere "outside" the pivot table, the pivot table editor will be hidden. Here's the final output:

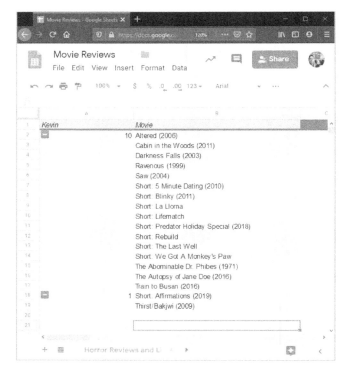

The Final Pivot Table

That shows sixteen ten out of ten films, and only two stinkers. I think he's being generous!

Still, that pivot table is now done. As we add more movies to the original spreadsheet each week, this list will update automatically, merging in the new information as needed. If I were to create a column in the original data containing the "Year Reviewed," I would then also be able to filter out the films from 2018, 2019, 2020, and so on.

It's extremely useful, and nothing I've done here affects the layout or appearance of the original data in any way. If you highlight a cell in your pivot table and start mashing on the keyboard, your data is untouched. It's really nice!

Randomize range takes a selected range of cells and shuffles them. The values don't change, but their positions within the range shift. For example, if you had five selected cells with the values 1,2,3,4, and 5 and randomized them, you might get the same cells with the values 3,5,1,2, and 4. You get the same numbers, but their positions are "scrambled."

Named ranges Select a range of cells and choose this option to "Name" a range of cells. This name can then be used in place of the cell addresses in most functions and references. Going back to our example with the two stores, I could select cells B2 to B8 and name them Store_1 and then select cells C2 to C8 and name them Store_2 (Note that you cannot have spaces in a named range). Then, anywhere in the worksheet, I can reference that range. For example, I could use the function =SUM(Store_1) instead of =SUM(A2:A8). This is an especially useful feature if you access data on other Sheets than the one onscreen.

Protect sheets and ranges Google Sheets is a powerful tool for collaboration with others. Once in a while, you may want users of a spreadsheet to be able to enter data in one place but not to be able to change other things, as opposed to giving them read-only access. For example, you may want to allow anyone to enter today's sales data for their store, but you don't want them to be able to change the formulas for figuring sums, averages, etc. You have the option to protect entire sheets or just certain ranges within sheets.

Once again using our "Two Stores" example, we want to allow the store managers to be able to enter their sales information for the various days for their stores, but not to be able to change the Sum formulas or the days of the week. Select the days of the week (A2 to A8) and choose "Protect cells and ranges" from the Data menu.

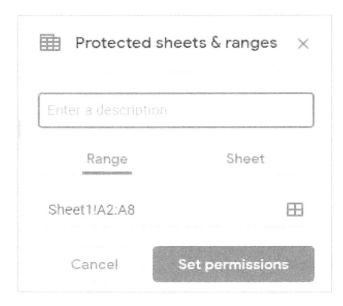

Protect Range

You can enter a description like "Days of the week" if you like, or you can leave the description blank. The important thing is the range "Sheet1!A2:A8." If you click on "Set permissions," you'll get something like the following:

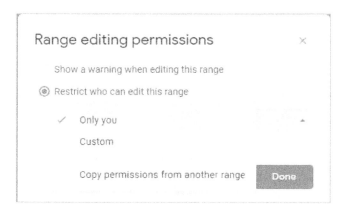

Set Permissions Dialog

And your options now are "Only you," aka the creator/maintainer of the spreadsheet, or "Custom," where you can choose from a list of the people with whom the sheet is shared. For the days of the week, no one needs to change that but you, so you would choose "Only you."

Next, you would select the two "Sum" cells, B9 and C9, and do the same thing; no one should be able to change those cells but you.

Now, the interesting part. With the cells for Store 1, you want the store manager for Store 1 and Store 2 to be able to enter their own sales figures, but only for their own stores. You could set the permission for cells B2 to B8 to the store manager for Store 1 and cells C2 to C8 to the store manager for Store 2. You would also make sure that **you** have permission to change these, in case corrections are needed at some point. This way, the Store 1 manager (or you) can alter the numbers only in the seven cells pertaining to their store and nowhere else, and the Store 2 manager can do the same, but only with their store.

A different way to do the same thing is by protecting the whole sheet. Just select "Protected sheets and ranges" as before, without anything selected. This time, click on the "Sheet" tab:

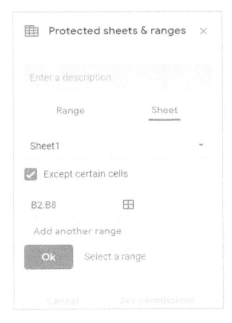

Protect sheet

This essentially denies anyone from being able to change anything at all on the sheet. If you choose "Except certain cells," then you can allow permission to edit a specific range, like B2:B8 for the manager of Store 1 and C2:C8 for store manager 2.

Whether you choose to protect specific ranges or entire sheets with exceptions depends on the complexity of the sheet and what you need, but either way, it's a very useful tool for spreadsheets that involve collaboration.

Split text to columns Lets you take the text entered in a cell and split it up into various columns automatically. When you choose this option from the menu, a drop-down menu will appear, allowing you to choose what character Google Sheets will use as a delimiter, i.e. what character goes between each item in your list. This can be a comma, semicolon, period, space, or some custom character that you enter. This feature can be used to populate a spreadsheet from some kind of user-entered data that isn't exactly in the right format.

For one use-case example, this is handy when you have a list of names and you want to split them into first name in one column and last name in another column. If you have a list that looks like this:

```
Brian Schell
Bob Jones
Joe Jones
```

Then you could split the data up by using the "space" delimiter. Likewise, if the list looks like this:

```
Schell, Brian
Jones, Bob
Jones, Joe
```

Then you could use the "Comma" delimiter to break up the names into columns.

Remove duplicates takes a selected range and looks through the range for duplicate values and removes them. For example, a list like this:

1
2
2
2
3
4
4
5

Would be shortened to:

1
2
3
4
5

All the unique values are retained, and the duplicates are deleted (and the cells are shifted up).

Note that if you choose more than one column in your range, each entire row must match exactly. For example:

1, 2
2, 3
2, 3
2, 2

Would become:

1, 2
2, 3
2, 2

Even though the last three entries all began with the value "2", only the two rows in the middle matched exactly.

Trim whitespace simply takes the selected cells and removes any leading or trailing spaces from the data. It also removes any multiple spacing between words. It ignores single spaces between words.

Group / Ungroup allows you to collect a selection of rows or columns into "groups" which can be hidden or revealed as needed. Going back to the example with the two stores, we can group the seven days together by selecting rows 2-8. Once these are selected, click on "Group" in the Data menu. Once this is done, a grouping bracket appears in the left-hand margin next to those cells. There's a minus sign along that edge as well:

		A	B	C
	1		Store 1	Store 2
	2	Monday	$1,045.00	$0.00
	3	Tuesday	$600.00	$500.00
	4	Wednesday	$225.00	$600.00
	5	Thursday	$190.00	$400.00
	6	Friday	$1,045.00	$374.00
	7	Saturday	$300.00	$275.00
	8	Sunday	$0.00	$490.00
	9		$3,405.00	$2,639.00

Group exposed (see the - on the far left)

If you click on the minus sign, the group will "fold up." All the data is still there, and the totals on line 9 don't change, but all that daily data is now hidden:

		A	B	C	D
	1		Store 1	Store 2	
	9		$3,405.00	$2,639.00	
	10				
	11				

Group is hidden (see the + on the far left)

And of course, if you click on the + sign, the data all comes back. In this little example, this isn't all that useful, but if we had many months of data like this, it would be useful to be able to hide all those individual weeks.

Note that you can have multiple "nested" layers of groups as well. In our example, we hid a group of seven days. If we had four weeks in the month, each of those weeks could be a group, and then the month itself could be a "supergroup" containing the four weeks. That way, you could hide or expose entire months or specific weeks as needed.

If you make a mistake or decide that the group doesn't work, you can select the same rows or columns and click on "Ungroup" to reverse this. For some reason, "Undo" doesn't work with the grouping feature.

THE TOOLS MENU

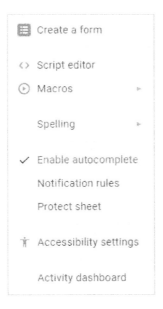

The Tools Menu

Create a form Google Forms are one of Google Sheet's most unique features. The Forms app allows you to create an online form, survey, questionnaire, test, or sign-up sheet that is available to anyone on the Internet. Once someone has filled out the form and clicked on the "Submit" button, the data from the form populates a spreadsheet in Google Sheets. When you choose to "Create a form," you get a new window that looks like this:

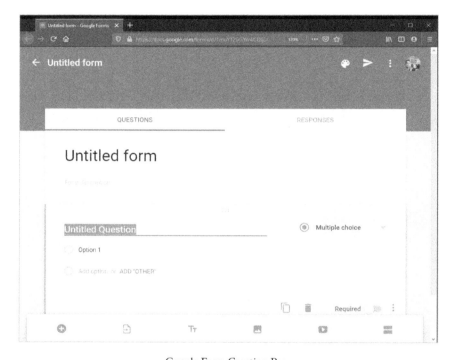

Google Form Creation Page

For example, just by filling in the blanks and creating a few checkboxes, you can have a nice survey form. Below, I have created a simple one-question multiple choice form:

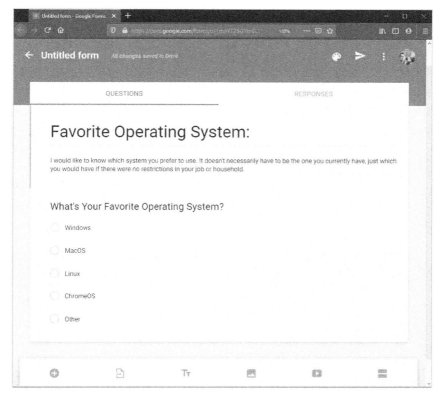

Simple Multiple-Choice Form

Script Editor The script editor exists to allow you to enter custom scripting code that does complex functions that aren't included in a Google Sheets. This is almost certainly something you don't want to get involved with as a beginner, but if you ever need Google Sheets to do something it wasn't really designed to do, then do a Google search for that function– it may be something that can be added here via the scripts editor or as an add-on under the "Add-ons" menu.

At the top of the screen, you can name your form. The "Palette" icon lets you customize the colors, fonts, and background image on the form. The "Airplane" icon lets you invite someone to take your test or survey. You can also use this dialog to invite collaborators, who will also have the ability to modify the form. The "three-dot" menu gives you access to an array of options, including the ability to preview and test the form, restrict each user to a single submission, move, copy, trash, print, and other actions you can take upon the form.

The buttons on the bottom are "Add Question," "Import Questions," "Add Title & Description," "Add Image," Add Video," and "Add Section." Using these tools, you can make an interactive test, questionnaire, application, or just about anything else that asks for information and records the answers. All of this work is done under the "Questions" tab.

On the other hand, under the "Responses" tab, we can decide what to do with our answers. If you do nothing special with the output of the form, you can see the results right here:

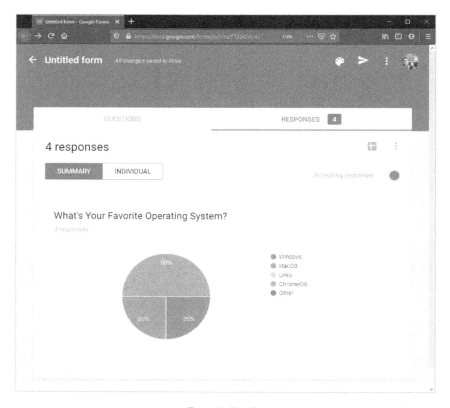

Example Results

Probably the most useful thing to do with a form is with the little green spreadsheet icon on the right-hand side of the screen. It allows you to place the results of the survey in a new or existing spreadsheet:

Select Destination for Results

If you want the results of the form to go into a blank spreadsheet, then you should choose the first option, otherwise, choose an existing spreadsheet. If you choose to create a new spreadsheet, you'll see something like the following:

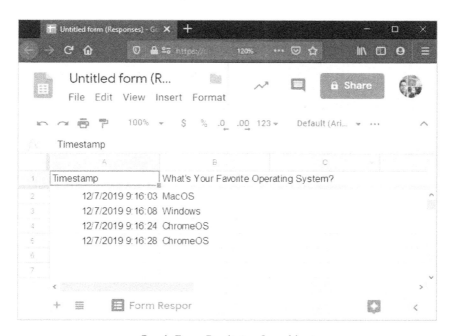

Google Forms Results in a Spreadsheet

... and then you can add in functions to count, summarize, graph, or otherwise manipulate that data. Of course, this example has only one question and only four responses, but there's really no limit to how complex these forms can be.

Macros - Record Macros allows you to record a sequence of keystrokes that can be named and repeated. Once you have recorded a sequence of keystrokes, you can save them with a name and keyboard combination (usually Ctrl-Alt-Shift-Number). Much like the Script Editor, this is a complex and much more power-user style tool.

- *Manage Macros* allows you to edit, delete, rename, or change the keystroke combination of the macros you've already created. It should be fairly straightforward to change the keystroke combination or the name, but if you click on the three dots next to the macro name, you can edit or delete the code (via the script editor) that represents the macro.
- *Import Macros* allows you to write a script in the Script Editor and assign it to a macro keystroke combination.
- *Others* After you have created one or more macros, you will see them listed in the menu beneath "Import Macros" and you can choose them from the menu using the keyboard or mouse in addition to using the assigned keystrokes.

Spelling Has two submenus:

- *Spell Check* goes through your document and checks for spelling errors against Google Sheet's dictionary. If misspelled words are found, Sheets will ask you what to do with the word. You have the option to correct the word to Sheets' suggested replacement, you can ignore the error, or you can add the word to your personal dictionary. If you add the word to your personal dictionary, it will be saved permanently and will not be flagged as a typo in the future.
- *Personal Dictionary* lets you manage what's in your personal dictionary. You can add, delete, or view words in the list. If

you accidentally add a word to your dictionary and then decide to change or remove it, this is how you do that.

Enable Autocomplete is a simple checkbox that is either on or off. Autocomplete will look at what you are typing and try to finish your words for you. If you are trying to enter a function and don't remember the entire function, just start typing, and a drop-down list of suggestions will appear. You can then hit the spacebar if the function you want is highlighted, or you can select it with the arrow keys or mouse if you can see it on the list.

Notification Rules is mostly used for sheets that have collaborators. You can set this feature to notify you if:

- Any changes are made to the sheet itself
- Anyone submits a form
- And you also have the option of getting notified at the time of your choosing:
- Once a day with a "Daily Digest" email
- Right away, as soon as the change above is noticed.

Protect Sheet is the same as the Protected Ranges/Protected Sheets mentioned under the View Menu. You can set who has the permission to modify a range of cells or an entire sheet. As with many other features, this is primarily only useful for collaborate/multiuser Sheets.

Accessibility Settings is useful if you need screen reader or Braille hardware support. Turn on the feature here but check out the "Learn More" link on the dialog box to see specific instructions on how to interface with your particular screen reader or Braille hardware.

If you turn on the accessibility features, a new main-level menu, "Accessibility," will appear to the right of the "Help" menu. This menu allows you to have the software read aloud to you in various ways. It can read rows, columns, single cells, comments, and various other options.

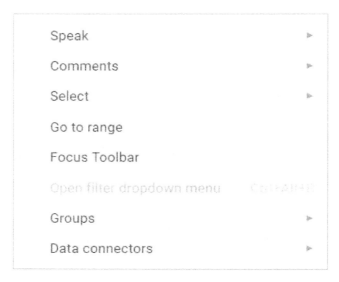

Accessibility Menu

Activity Dashboard Tells you about the activity of your collaborators. The five icons on the left side of the popup dialog allow you to choose to:

- See who is using the sheet currently.
- See the history of how many people accessed the document.
- The comments they entered.
- The sharing activity, if any.
- To allow document editors and owners to see the history (or keep it private).

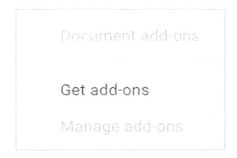

Add-ons Menu

ADD-ONS MENU

This menu is for adding extra functions to Google Sheets by installing plugins published by third-party developers. There are hundreds of these, and I've only tried a few.

If you click on "Get add-ons...," you'll be taken to the Google Web store, where you can browse what's available and install the things that interest you. It's the same process as installing new apps on a Chromebook.

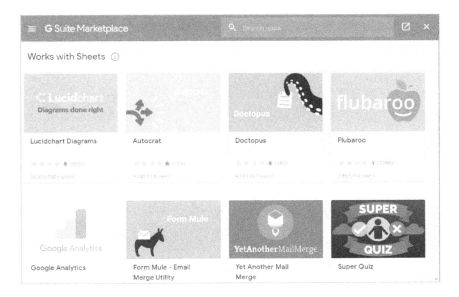

Google Web Store, Looking for Add-Ons

There's an add-on I found called "Autocrat." It's an add-on that allows the user to create nice-looking PDF files and merge data from the spreadsheet into the text on the page. It's essentially an enhanced "mail-merge" function. I want to use this, so on the store page, I will click on the blue button that says, "Individual Install," and follow the installation steps that appear on the screen.

Note that if you are a Domain Administrator, you will also have the option for "Domain Install," which will install the selected add-on for everyone in the organization. Circumstances vary; some things you may want to let everyone use, while others may be tools just for your own use, so be careful which installation method you choose.

You will often have to grant various permissions to access your Sheets with these add-ons. That's a normal thing, but keep in mind that it is conceivably possible that some of the apps *could* be *malicious* in some way. Google screens all the apps and add-ons on their store, but they are **not** super-thorough about it. Just use a little caution when installing apps from unknown sources.

So, after I have installed the Autocrat add-on, I can access it by pulling down the Tools menu, which now looks like this:

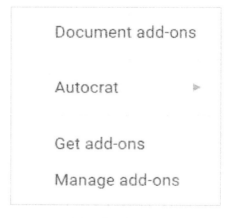

Altered Tools Menu

As you can see, the menu has changed to show the new add-on. If you install something from the Google Web Store, you can use **Manage add-ons...** to delete it if it's not what you wanted.

Some add-ons are very simple things, and others are extremely complex. Once you start adding to Sheets, anything is possible!

There's a list of my ten favorite add-ons later on in the book.

HELP

The top line of the Help menu is a search bar. This is for finding specific things within the menus. If you can't remember how to find the option for "Full screen," for example, you can start typing that in, and as you type, it will narrow down your options. It's way faster than hunting through all the menus for something you *know* is there... *somewhere*.

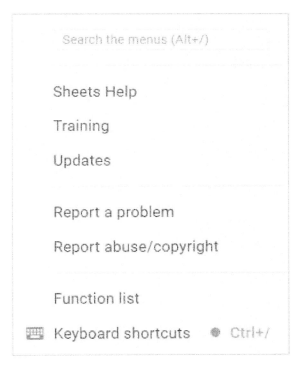

Help Menu

Sheets Help This one brings up a dialog box that lets you search very comprehensive help files for what you need. There's a lot more in this documentation than just menu items. One of the benefits about Google Sheets being a cloud-based system is that when Google makes changes to the way some feature works, they update the documentation at the same time.

Training offers numerous ways to learn and improve how you work with Sheets. There is a link to a free online course through the website Coursera, as well as cheat sheets, productivity guides, tips, and a lot more. The book in your hand is meant to be an overview of the possibilities and an introduction to what Google Sheets can do, but to get "down in the weeds," you should probably take a look at some of the **very** in-depth resources that Google has linked to here.

Updates Brings up a dialog that loads in a list of recent updates to the software. Google adds something new, some new feature or fix, nearly every month, and if you check in here every so often, it will keep you up to date on what they've added. Because Google Sheets is completely cloud-based, you don't have to *do* anything to update the software, it just happens when Google makes it happen, but this way you can stay on top of it:

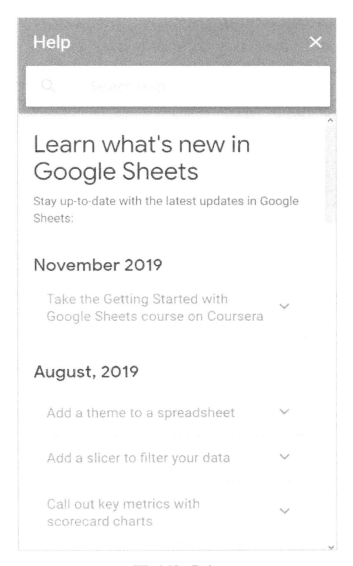

What's New Dialog

Report a problem Brings up a dialog where you can type a technical problem, and this even lets you (optionally) include a screenshot of what's on your screen so they can see the problem. This is here specifically to help Google fix bugs, so don't expect direct help with your problem by using this.

Report abuse/copyright If someone has shared a file with you that is illegal or otherwise wildly inappropriate, this is a way to report that.

Function List is exactly what it sounds like: a complete list of all the math/formula functions that are supported by Google Sheets.

Type ▲	Name	Syntax	Description
Array	ARRAY_CONSTRAIN	ARRAY_CONSTRAIN(input_range, num_rows, num_cols)	Constrains an array result to a specified size. Learn more ☐
Array	FREQUENCY	FREQUENCY(data, classes)	Calculates the frequency distribution of a one-column array into specified classes. Learn more ☐
Array	GROWTH	GROWTH(known_data_y, [known_data_x], [new_data_x], [b])	Given partial data about an exponential growth trend, fits an ideal exponential growth trend and/or predicts further values. Learn more ☐
Array	LINEST	LINEST(known_data_y, [known_data_x], [calculate_b], [verbose])	Given partial data about a linear trend, calculates various parameters about the ideal linear trend using the least-squares method. Learn more ☐

Function List

Each function (and there are hundreds) is listed with its category, name, the necessary syntax and required arguments, as well as a description, often with a "Learn More" link. At the top of the list is a search box along with the capability to narrow down the list by the type of functions. Everything you could ever want is in this list... somewhere.

Keyboard shortcuts This is a list, organized by category, of all the various keyboard shortcut combinations that are available to you. There are a large number of them and learning at least some of these will help you work faster. Working with the keyboard is always faster than using the mouse/trackpad. There is a list of keyboard shortcuts for use with the Chromebook keyboard later in this book. For Windows or Mac keyboard shortcuts, take a look at the online help.

GOOGLE SHEETS TOOLBAR

The Toolbar is located right under the menu bar and just above the main document window. Although it changes depending on what you are doing, most of the time, it looks like this:

The Toolbar

From left to right, there are "groups" of icons separated by small vertical dividers. They are (in order from right to left):

- **Undo**
- **Redo**
- **Print**
- **Paint format**

- **Zoom**

- **Format as currency**
- **Format as percent**
- **Decrease decimal places**
- **Increase decimal places**
- **More (number) formats**

———

- **Font name**
- **Font size**
- **Bold**
- **Italic**
- **Strikethrough**

———

- **Fill color**
- **Borders**
- **Merge Cells**

———

- **Horizontal Align**
- **Vertical Align**
- **Text wrapping**
- **Text Rotation**

- **Insert link**
- **Insert comment**
- **Insert chart**
- **Create a Filter**
- **Functions**
- and the little "caret" on the far right **hides the menu bar**, giving you more space.

We've already covered most of these function as accessed through the menus, but there are a few new things here:

Paint format This is an easy, but often-forgotten tool for copying styles, colors, and font attributes. If you need to reproduce the look of one cell somewhere else, this is for you. Take a selected cell, set it with bold, italic, underline, coloring, styles, or most other visual options. Next, you select that cell and then click Paint format and click or select the target cell(s). The target cell's formatting now matches the original selection. This is especially useful if you've got some complex formatting that changes in several places.

Number formats allow you to "describe" what kind of number is in a cell or range of cells. There are common ones already on the toolbar for currency and percent, but by pulling down the menu, there are another dozen number formats you can choose from:

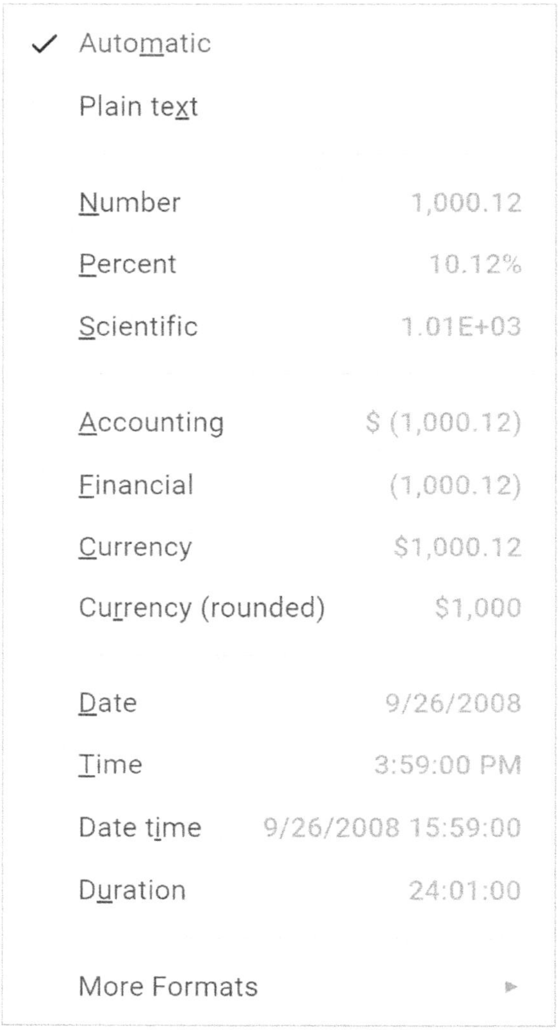

✓ Automatic	
Plain text	
Number	1,000.12
Percent	10.12%
Scientific	1.01E+03
Accounting	$ (1,000.12)
Financial	(1,000.12)
Currency	$1,000.12
Currency (rounded)	$1,000
Date	9/26/2008
Time	3:59:00 PM
Date time	9/26/2008 15:59:00
Duration	24:01:00
More Formats	▶

Number Formats

You can also use the Increase/Decrease Decimal button to display your numbers with more or less precision. If the supplied number formatting options still aren't what you are looking for, you can click on "More Formats" at the bottom of the menu and design your own number format, as shown below. Note that the scrollable list given simply shows you examples, but you can modify them however you want.

Custom number formats	
0	Apply
Sample: 1235	Help
0	1235
0.00	1234.56
#,##0	1,235
#,##0.00	1,234.56
#,##0_);(#,##0)	1,235
#,##0_);[Red](#,##0)	1,235
#,##0.00_);(#,##0.00)	1,234.56
#,##0.00_);[Red](#,##0.00)	1,234.56

Custom Number Formats

Fonts You change fonts in Sheets the same way you do in any word processor. You highlight some text, pull down the fonts drop-down list, and pick the one you want. The five most recently used fonts appear at the top of the list, and then the rest appear in an alphabetical list.

Google offers only the most commonly used fonts by default, but there are many, many more available to you. At the top of the list is an option for "More fonts..." which brings up the following dialog box:

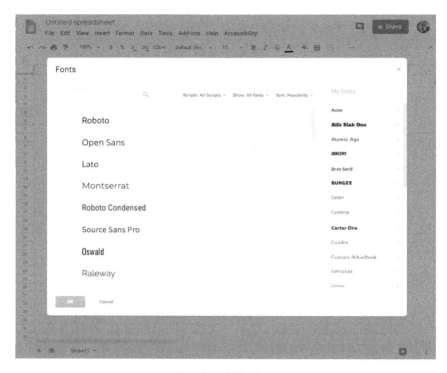

List of Available Fonts

The list on the left shows all the available options from Google. There are hundreds, if not thousands, of possible fonts available. Scroll to the bottom of the visible list, and more appear. You can also type in the name of a font into the search bar or sort the list in various ways by using the drop-down menus at the top of the screen. In the right-most pane, you can see the list of extra fonts that you have added to your Chromebook. Remember that Google Sheets is a cloud app that runs only in a web browser, so it can *only* use the fonts that Google supplies. The fonts you may have already installed on your Windows or Mac computers are not available to you here.

Font size All font measurements are in points (72 per inch). The sizes can be chosen from the drop-down list, or if the size you want isn't listed, you can type any number into the box at the top of the list. Points (abbreviated *pts* in most apps) are one of those things that we see all the time but are rarely explained. Points are the size measurement for fonts and spacing. Most Google Sheets documents default to using the Arial font, and set it to a size of 10 points. If you've ever changed a font, you've probably changed that little number next to it to adjust the size. That size is measured in points. But what is a point?

Back in the early days of the printing press, each individual character was made of lead, and a printed document would take hundreds or thousands of individual little character pieces assembled together to make a plate. For some reason, the letters that were one inch tall were deemed to be 72 points high. That's generally the basis for fonts even today. If you set a font to 72 points, it (should) print at around one inch tall. A font at 36 points should print at a half-inch tall, and 12-point type should be ⅙ of an inch. This isn't strictly true anymore because of lots of variables in computers, font choices, and printers, but generally speaking, that's what the point system is all about.

Font Color and **Fill Color** allow you to select the colors. The letter "A" with the underline allows you to choose the color of the value inside a cell or range. The spilled-paint-bucket button allows you to choose the background color of the cell itself.

Borders can be tricky to get the hang of at first, but once you catch on, you can create all kinds of fancy layouts, and even design paper forms with them:

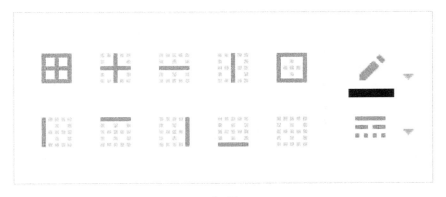

Border Menu

Clicking on the various icons will darken the edges of a cell (or range of cells). You can make a line at the top edge, bottom edge, right or left edge of any cell. You can make a big rectangle around a group of boxes or fill in a whole grid of lines. The pencil icon allows you to choose a color for the border lines, and the dotted lines below the pencil are for choosing dashed, dotted, or other patterns of lines. Note that when you change colors, lines that you have already drawn do not change; only the currently selected cells will become that new color.

Merge cells is greyed out unless you have more than one cell selected. If you highlight two or more cells and click this icon, you will have the choice to merge them horizontally into one wide cell, or vertically for one tall cell. Not all your cells need to be the same size!

Horizontal Align allows you to line up the contents in the cell along the left or right margin or to center it in the middle of the cell. This works the same as the alignment controls in nearly any word processor.

Vertical Align is a little different than the previous option. Since cells in a spreadsheet can be any size, you also have the option of aligning the contents of a cell vertically, along the top or bottom edge, or vertically in the middle of the cell. Between these last two options, you can position your text and numbers anywhere inside a cell.

Text Wrapping shows a small dropdown box with three icons that determines what happens when there is too much text to fit in a cell horizontally. All of these are changes in on-screen visual appearance only and do not change the values of the selected (or any adjacent) cells:

- *Overflow* lets the long text run over into the next cell. Visually, the contents of the cell may cover or obscure text in the cell to the right.
- *Wrap* makes the long text wrap to the next line and makes the cell expand vertically to fit the text.
- *Clip* simply visually chops off the end of the text, making the cell to the right completely visible.

Text Rotation lets you change the angle at which text is displayed. Normally, text runs from left to right just like in a book. It can, however, run vertically up or down, or at any angle you prefer.

There are buttons in the toolbar to make the text tilt upwards or downwards at either 45- or 90-degree angles and either "Rotate" or "Stack" the individual letters. If you need a more precise tilt/rotation, the final option in the Text Rotation toolbar lets you enter a value in degrees.

Insert Link allows you to insert a link to another cell or sheet in the file, a different file, or a website. You can paste in a web link or use the dialog box to select some other location within the sheet.

Insert Comment was discussed previously in the section "Google Sheets Commands and Menus" and also under the section for the Insert menu. This toolbar button does the same thing. It allows you to include a comment that can be used using the various "Show Comment" options.

Insert Chart is the same as the "Insert Chart" function under the Insert menu.

Create Filter allows you to change what rows can be seen in your spreadsheet.

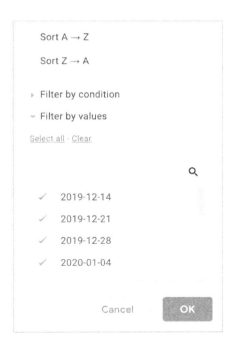

Create Filter Dialog

You can simply use this feature to simply sort the table by value, either ascending or descending. More powerfully, you can also "Filter by Condition," which hides all cells that don't meet criteria that you choose:

None

Is empty

Is not empty

Text contains

Text does not contain

Text starts with

Text ends with

Text is exactly

Date is

Date is before

Date is after

Greater than

Greater than or equal to

Less than

Less than or equal to

Is equal to

Is not equal to

Is between

Is not between

Custom formula is

Filter by Condition

For example, you could choose to hide any data where the Date "is before" this year. Or where the Sales value is "Less than" $100. You can also create "Custom Formula" conditions. This feature works similarly to the Conditional Formatting feature we saw in the Data menu. While conditional formatting would color or otherwise make some data stand out, this hides the row completely. Filtering is extremely powerful, and also fairly complex, and Google has included a "Learn More" link in the drop-down menu for this item with several good videos on the possibilities.

Formula Button gives you quick access to the most used spreadsheet functions. SUM, AVERAGE, COUNT, MAX, and MIN are pinned right to the top, since these are the most commonly used functions, but hundreds of other functions are found in the menus below them. There is, of course, a "Learn More" link at the bottom of the menu.

Hide/Show menu bar This is the little "caret" (^) that appears on the far right of the toolbar. This either points up or down, and either shows or hides the "heading" portion of the Google Sheets interface. This helps reduce "clutter" and lets you go for a more distraction-free interface.

Show side panel This is the little < or > at the bottom-right of the screen. This expands or collapses the side panel, which includes several mini-apps that open in a side-pane. You can open Google Calendar, Google Keep, or Google Tasks in small windowed views. Google Calendar gives you your appointments and schedule for today or for the month. Google Keep is a great little note-taking app. None of these are actually a part of Google Sheets, as they are external apps, so we won't get into them here.

Part Two

GOOGLE SHEETS TIPS AND WORKFLOWS

TIPS AND WORKFLOWS

*W*e've gone through all the menus, buttons, and toolbars that Google Sheets has to offer, so now you know all the major features that Sheets has to offer. That still doesn't really give the whole picture, however, as it's hard to know how to take advantage of a lot of those features. This is a list of important concepts, tools, and ideas that don't fit in elsewhere in the book:

QUICKLY ADDING LINKS WITHIN A DOCUMENT

If you want to insert a link to some internal heading within your document or to an external website, just highlight a word or phrase and then right-click with a mouse (or two-finger click on the trackpad), and a context menu will appear. One of the options in the menu is **Link...** An even faster way is to highlight the text and hit *ctrl-k*. Either way, the link menu appears, and what it shows varies depending on what you've selected.

You can choose one of the options that Google gives you, or you can enter your own URL or choose a cell or range of cells within your document. There are lots of options for internal and external linking.

All of these will appear in your document as blue underlined text, which you can recolor or restyle if you prefer.

EXPORTING AND GETTING DOCUMENTS OUT OF GOOGLE SHEETS

At some point, you're going to actually finish creating your document, and you'll want to do something with it. Many internal documents that are shared collaboratively never actually need to be exported, but sometimes, you just need a printout or Excel-compatible file.

Emailing Documents

If you want to email the document, that's easy. Go to the **File** menu, choose **Email as attachment...** and fill in the "To," "Subject," and "Message" as needed. The drop-down box allows you to choose to send your document in various formats, including Microsoft Excel (.xlsx) and Portable Document Format (.pdf) formats. You can also choose to paste the document into the text of the email rather than as an attachment. Sheets will send the email with your Gmail account as the sender.

Downloading Files

If you just want a file to backup, email later, copy to a flash drive, or whatever, then go to **File** > **Download As...** and choose an appropriate file type. The list of format includes Microsoft Excel (.xlsx), Portable Document Format (.pdf), comma- or tab-separated Values (.tsv or .csv), open document (.ods), or as a zipped file including HTML and all images.

Publishing to the Web

Another option is to publish your document as a page on the web. To do this, go to **File** > **Publish to the web...** and choose from the various options that are presented. You can use a text link that can be emailed or posted online so that anyone can read your document. If you prefer, you can instead embed your document within another page. Depending on what you want to do, this can be a really powerful way to get a message or document "out there."

Share the Document

We've talked about collaboration already, but under **File** > **Sharing...** you can also get a link to send someone that will allow them to access your spreadsheet. You can choose whether the person "Can edit," "Can comment," or "Can view." People who "Can view" can only read, not change or affect the document in any way.

Copy and Paste

This method isn't recommended, as sometimes formatting can be lost with complex documents, but it's usually possible to simply highlight the entire document (use ctrl-a to make this easy), then **Edit** > **Copy**. Then open up whatever Excel (or any similar app) and use that app's **Paste** function to drop that text into the other app. This method generally works with anything that will allow you to paste text, but keep in mind that some apps will not allow you to paste pictures, formatting, and links; it's often a text-only paste. It just depends on the target app.

INSTANT COLLABORATION

Google Sheets offers several different ways to collaborate, but here is the simplest way to get started:

1. Create a Spreadsheet and save it with a filename.
2. Click on the green "Share" button in the top right-hand corner of the screen.
3. Enter one or more emails for your collaborators, separating them with commas. You can add a note explaining the

purpose of your email as well; something like, "Hey, Collaborate with me on this!" If you click the "pencil" icon, you can also choose for the collaborators to only be able to read or comment on your document, but not edit it.

4. The people you email will get an email that looks similar to the screenshot below.

5. At this point, the other people can open and edit your document.

6. If more than one person is accessing the document at one time, each person's text cursor will show up in a different color, labelled with that person's name. Everyone can be working on the same document at the same time, writing text, deleting text, and leaving comments. It's very useful and actually pretty fun as well.

Email Containing an Invitation to Edit

ENABLE OFFLINE EDITING

One of the arguments people use as an excuse to "hate on" Chromebooks is that you can't use them offline. This hasn't been true in many years. In order to setup offline Sheets access, follow these steps when you do have Internet access:

1. You must use the Google Chrome browser and must not be using private browsing.
2. Install and turn on the Google Docs Offline Chrome extension, which can be found at (or searched for, since it's all entered in one really long line):
   https://chrome.google.com/webstore/detail/google-docs-offline/ghbmnnjooekpmoecnnnilnnbdlolhkhi
3. Make sure you have enough available space on your device to save your files.
4. Open Chrome and make sure you're signed into Chrome.
5. Go to **drive.google.com/drive/settings**. It should look similar to the image below.
6. Check the box next to "Sync Google Docs, Sheets, Slides & Drawings files to this computer so that you can edit offline."

Settings Screen

Depending on how many documents you have, it may take a little while to download all your documents the first time. At this point, your files should load and be editable even without the Internet. Once you return to a place with an Internet connection, everything should synchronize with the cloud version of the document.

USING GOOGLE SHEETS AND GOOGLE SLIDES WITHIN DOCS

Google Sheets is Google's spreadsheet solution, great for tables and graphs, while Slides is their presentation/slideshow option. They compete with the better-known Excel and PowerPoint. Google Docs is the equivalent word processing app. These three apps are carefully designed to work together, and they all allow aspects of each one to be embedded or accessed within the other two. Sometimes, it's helpful to embed a table, graphic, or slide into your written Docs and vice-versa.

Creating a new chart from scratch within Docs is surprisingly easy. Just pull down the "Insert" menu and choose "Chart" along with the style of chart you want. The system will insert a generic-looking chart of that type and also create a Google Sheets spreadsheet with the same name as your current document. If you edit that spreadsheet, you can change the labels, value, or add new categories. As you make changes, they will be reflected in the chart.

Here is the spreadsheet that Google creates for the "Pie chart" option:

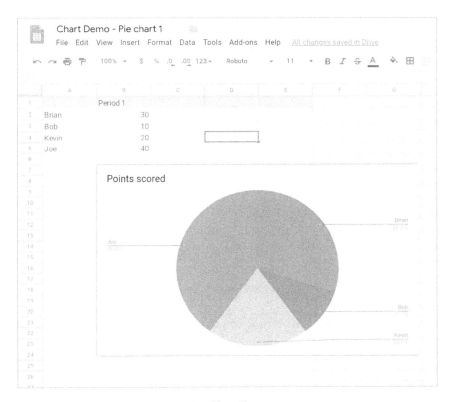

Pie Chart Sheet

And here is the resulting document in the Docs app:

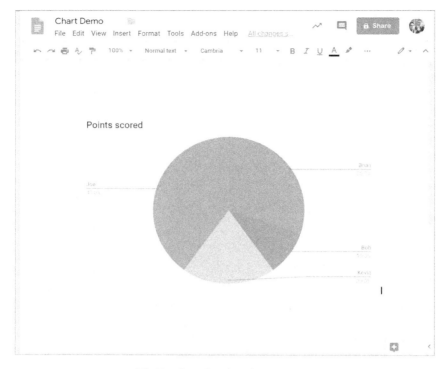

The Resulting Graph in the Document

So as you can see, the data and graph in the spreadsheet are linked into the word-processing document. You can also do something similar with already-made spreadsheets using the *Insert menu*'s **Insert chart** feature.

EMBEDDING A SPREADSHEET WITHIN DOCS OR SLIDES

1. Open a sheet in Google Sheets in Google Chrome
2. Select the cells you want to put in Docs or Slides.
3. Pull down the Edit menu and then choose "Copy."
4. Now open a document or presentation in Google Docs or Google Slides.
5. Click where you want to put your table and from the Edit menu, choose "Paste."

6. Choose "Link to spreadsheet" or "Paste unlinked" and click Paste.

SPARKLINES

Sparklines appear in only a single cell. The idea with Sparklines is to show simple trends, not detailed information. In a single cell, use the function

`=SPARKLINE(data, options)`

The "data" can be a range or a list of values. There are many options including the type of chart (line, bar, column, or win-loss), and numerous functions pertaining to appearance.

Here's an example:

	A	B	C	D	E	F	G	H
1	Monday	Tuesday	Wednesday	Thursday	Friday	Saturday	Sunday	Trend
2	$100.00	$200.00	$300.00	$400.00	$100.00	$200.00	$400.00	
3								

Sparkline example

The cells A2:G2 have some sales numbers. The cell in H2 contains the function

`=SPARKLINE(A2:G2)`

And you can see the tiny little line graph that results in cell H2. If you have lots of rows of data, you can have a sparkline chart at the end of each line. They don't take up a lot of room, and they're very attractive, since you can customize the size, style, color, and lots more on these little trend lines.

ADD IMAGES TO YOUR SPREADSHEET

You can add images in most graphics formats to your sheet. This can be especially useful for including something like a company logo in your presentations and reports. Just use the function

`=IMAGE(url, mode, height, width)`

Where *url* is the URL of the image, including protocol (e.g. http://).

The value for url must either be enclosed in quotation marks or be a reference to a cell containing the appropriate text. For example,

`=IMAGE("http://bluehousebooks.com/wp-content/up-loads/2013/10/Blue-House-Logo.jpg")`

Note that there are optional arguments for image sizing.

TRANSLATIONS

Google has a language translation service that integrates well with Sheets. There's a function that will translate words in one language to another:

`=GOOGLETRANSLATE("je ne sais quoi","fr","en")`

As you can see, the first argument is the text (or a reference to a cell containing text), the second is the source (or "from") language, and the third argument is the destination ("to") language.

FULLSCREEN MODE

Between the toolbars in Sheets and whatever data you are using, sometimes the clutter of the browser gets to be a bit much. Under the View menu is the option for "Fullscreen." This hides the menus at the top of the screen— everything above the formula bar vanishes, giving you more room to work and less clutter for your eyeballs. Just hit the 'ESC' key to make everything go back to normal.

DON'T SAVE YOUR WORK

This is one of the most terrifying things. Have you *ever* exited out from an app and forgotten to save your work? Most of us have at one time or another, but that's not an issue with any of the Google Apps. Everything automatically saves every few seconds. This isn't even a feature you need to switch on (or off); it's just the way the system works.

OTHER USEFUL FUNCTIONS THAT IMPORT THINGS

Like the =IMAGE function above, there are other functions that you can use to load in data from the outside world. Here are two:

- **=GOOGLEFINANCE("AMZN","price",date(2019,12,20))** Imports the closing stock price for Amazon at close of business on December 20, 2019, using the AMZN stock symbol. If you do the stock market, you can import daily closing values for everything in your portfolio.
- **=IMPORTHTML("http://en.wikipedia.org/wiki/ Demographics_of_India", "table", 4)** Looks up data in a table or list somewhere out on the Internet from the URL of your choosing. In the example above, Sheets goes out and loads the Wikipedia page about India, and reports on the 4th Table included on the page.
- **=IMPORTXML(url, xpath_query)** For a more generic lookup-on-the-Internet feature, this one allows you to load XML, HTML, CSV, TSV, and RSS and ATOM XML feeds data from the web. The data is returned using an xpath query, which is beyond the scope of this book, but if you need to scrape an XML file, you probably know something about this already.

LINK TO ENTIRELY DIFFERENT SPREADSHEETS

You can easily link to locations and sheets within the file you're working on, but you can also like to entirely different spreadsheets in another file, or even someone else's account.

```
=IMPORTRANGE("https://docs.google.com/spread-
sheets/d/12345678901234567890", "Sheet1!A1:D12")
```

The example above connects to the spreadsheet at that URL and returns the data found on Sheet 1 within the range A1 through D12.

IF THIS THEN THAT

Google Sheets does a lot of things, but sometimes you want to interface with external tools even more than the functions above will allow. Tools like **IFTTT.com** (which stands for If This, Then That) are very useful in many cases. This service connects to various cloud-based apps and takes data from one web-app and sends it to another based on various conditions. This sounds complicated, but their system makes it all really easy. Here are a few of the functions that are just one or two clicks away:

Some of the automations available from IFTTT.com

JUST START TYPING

If you aren't sure about the exact syntax of a function, just start typing. If you know the first few letters of the function name, an autocomplete box with functions will appear to help you. You can choose between similarly named functions, and even the required and optional arguments will be displayed. Often, this help is enough to figure out exactly what you need to know. In the picture below, I remembered the function I wanted was called IMPORTHTML, but didn't remember what the arguments were. Help appears:

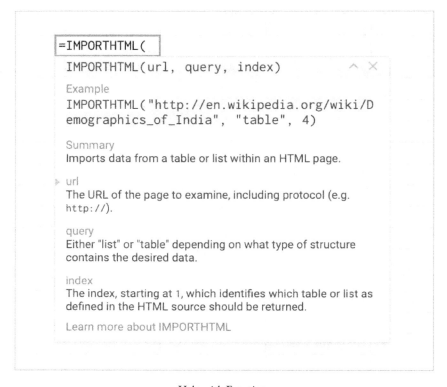

Help with Functions

And if that's not enough help to get you going, there's a link at the bottom of the little window to "Learn more about IMPORTHTML" which will take you right to the full help for the function.

TOP TEN ADD-ONS FOR GOOGLE SHEETS

We talked about Add-ons and how to install and use them back in the section about the Add-on menu. The Google Web Store contains a large number of add-ons and extensions, but I've listed some of the most useful and popular ones below. This is by far not all of them, and there may some here that don't interest you at all. If you have some kind of special application need that isn't built in to Google Sheets, always remember that the Add-ons are available. You may find exactly what you need. On the other hand, you may be perfectly happy using no add-ons at all. I know in my own case, I try to keep my tools as "clean" as possible and try to avoid add-ons if I can make the default tools work for me.

The list below has web store links which are easy to click if you are reading this book in ebook format, but difficult to use if you have the paperback. Sorry, there is no easy URL for add-ons. If you go to the Add-ons menu and choose "Get add-ons..." a dialog pops up with all the popular add-ons, but more useful is the search tool in the upper-right of that dialog. Just type in the name of the plug in and it shouldn't be too hard to find.

Autocrat

AUTOCRAT

Automate the creation and sharing of personalized documents with AutoCrat.

Autocrat is a document merge tool that allows you to take data from a spreadsheet and merge it into a document using a template. You can tell Autocrat which fields to merge via <<merge tags>> and then let Autocrat mass-generate personalized documents. You can optionally send the documents as email attachments as well. In addition, you can tell Autocrat to run when new forms are submitted, creating truly automated processes.

Website: **https://cloudlab.newvisions.org/**

Google Web Store:
https://gsuite.google.com/u/0/market-place/app/autocrat/539341275670

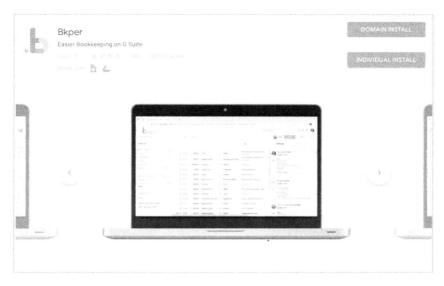

Bkper

BKPER

Bkper is a simple and robust collaborative double-entry bookkeeping platform that turns Google Sheets into a powerful accounting tool, with functions to easily create Balance Sheet and Profit & Loss statements, and connections to 10,000+ banks and credit cards institutions worldwide.

Website: **http://bkper.com**

Google Web Store:
https://gsuite.google.com/u/0/market-place/app/bkper/360398463400

Crop Sheet

CROP SHEET

Instead of deleting extra rows and columns yourself, simply crop the sheet to just the area you want to keep. Supports cropping to the data on the sheet or cropping to the cells you have selected.

Website: **None**

Google Web Store:
https://gsuite.google.com/u/0/market-place/app/crop_sheet/42816466715

Database Browser

DATABASE BROWSER

This "Database Browser" add-on provides an easy GUI for establishing connections with databases, browsing tables, and querying records out to Google Sheets.

Website: **http://jivrus.com**

Google Web Store:
https://gsuite.google.com/u/0/market-place/app/database_browser/480893432423

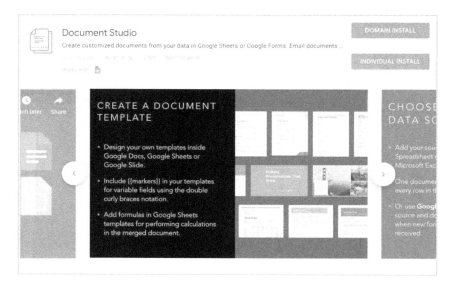

Document Studio

DOCUMENT STUDIO

Create documents from your spreadsheet data and Google Forms responses in a snap. Use built-in Mail Merge to email documents, files are saved in Google Drive, they can be automatically shared with colleagues or print them via Google Cloud Print. You can create documents in Google Drive and Team Drives.

Use Document Studio to create professional looking and sophisticated documents including personalized business letters, student test results, customer invoices, event tickets, vendor contracts, purchase orders, sales pitches and any other type of document that you need to generate on a repetitive basis. You'll never have to copy-paste data again.

Website: **https://digitalinspiration.com**

Google Web Store:
https://gsuite.google.com/u/0/market-place/app/document_studio/429444628321

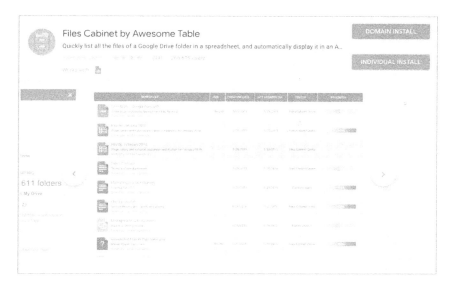

Files Cabinet

FILES CABINET

Files Cabinet by Awesome Table is an add-on that helps you list a Google Drive folder. It explores every child folder and lists every file that can be found. After giving you a quick count of all the folders and all the files, you get a list of the files that are ready to be displayed in a catalog created with Awesome Table.

Website: **http://sites.google.com/a/addonsfor-gapps.com/awesometableaddons**

Google Web Store: **https://gsuite.google.-com/u/0/marketplace/app/files_cabi-net_by_awesome_table/606635256305**

Fillable Documents for Sheets

FILLABLE DOCUMENT FOR SHEETS

The "Fillable Document for Sheets" add-on enhances the popular Fillable Document add-on by utilizing data from existing Google Sheets. Merge data from Google Sheets into Fillable Docs along with Fillable Document's creative feature of making a Google Doc as a LIVE FILLABLE FORM with the ability to store data into Google Sheets, generate merged document as Google Document & PDFs, deliver with templated email notifications. Also, Fillable Document can publish the document as fillable form, get the link or embed code to share with your users.

Fillable Document works as add-on on both Google Docs and Google Sheets.

Website: **http://jivrus.com**

Google Web Store:
https://gsuite.google.com/u/0/market-place/app/fillable_document_for_sheets/63828731146

Form Builder for Sheets

FORM BUILDER FOR SHEETS

"Form Builder for Sheets" helps you to build Google Forms in a very simple, fast way by importing fields/questions/quizzes from existing Google Sheets.

You do not need to pre-format your existing Google Sheet. Form Builder automatically identifies the questions and answers or quiz to import. This way, Form Builder works as an enhanced Form Creator.

Website: `http://jivrus.com`

Google Web Store:
`https://gsuite.google.com/u/0/market-place/app/form_builder_for_sheets/463417060578`

QR Code Generator

QR CODE GENERATOR

The QR Code Generator add-on lets you easily create QR codes from values in Google Spreadsheets. You can generate multiple QR codes by selecting a range of values in a spreadsheet. QR codes are saved either in a Google Document or as PNG files in Google Drive. This add-on is part of Mobile Attendance solution and customers can create employee ID cards containing QR codes.

Website: **http://attendance.mobi**

Google Web Store:
https://gsuite.google.com/u/0/market-place/app/qr_code_generator/771094986501

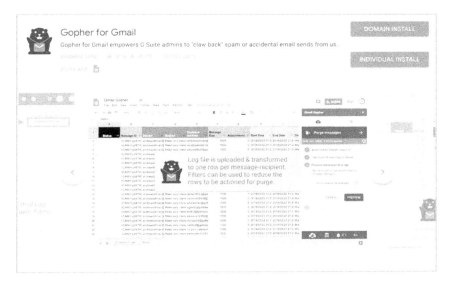

Gopher for Gmail

GOPHER FOR GMAIL

Recover emails after phishing attacks, FERPA breaches, or inappropriate sends...

Gmail, like any email system, can be a vector for malware and phishing attacks. While Google has gotten better at catching these threats before they arrive in user inboxes, the threat continues to evolve and occasionally evade auto-detection.

Whether it's a phishing attack, a FERPA snafu, or an inappropriate prank, school administrators need the power to remediate and quickly eliminate the threats posed by certain emails.

Website: **None**

Google Web Store:
`https://gsuite.google.com/u/0/market-place/app/gopher_for_gmail/244635294303`

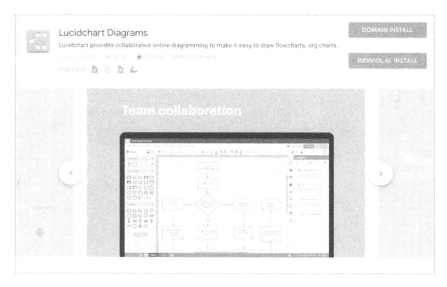

Lucid Chart

LUCIDCHART

Lucidhart is the #1 visual productivity platform for teams. Collaborate in real time to create flowcharts, ERDs, BPMN diagrams, wireframes, mockups, network diagrams, org charts, and more. Try industry-leading features such as data linking, diagram automation, and links and layers for interactive diagrams. Start your free trial today!

Lucidchart offers enterprise-grade security through AWS, SSO, and SAML integrations and domain lockdown to ensure your data remains safe and secure. Over 13 million users—including Google, DocuSign, Delta, Visa, Toyota, and Procter & Gamble—choose Lucidchart to quickly create professional, interactive diagrams documenting any process or idea. Connect Lucidchart to Google Drive, Docs, Sheets, Slides, and other industry-leading applications.

Still using Visio? Lucidchart's Visio import and export options make the transition painless. Not only is Lucidchart easier to use—it's more affordable. You can also import your files from draw.io, Gliffy, and Omnigraffle.

Website: `http://www.lucidchart.com`

Google Web Store:
`https://gsuite.google.com/u/0/market-place/app/lucidchart_diagrams/7081045131`

KEYBOARD SHORTCUTS

The following list of keyboard shortcuts is for any Chromebook. If you are running Google Sheets on Windows or Mac, the shortcuts are mostly the same, but the modifier keys change, for example, The Windows Key on PC, and Option and Command on Mac. If you aren't running a Chromebook, you can find all the keyboard commands at:

https://support.google.com/docs/answer/179738

As I mentioned previously, you certainly don't need to remember or use all of these, but you can save yourself a lot of time by learning at least some of them. If there's a task you find yourself doing repeatedly, for example, copy and pasting, it's going to be a lot faster to hit CTRL-C and CTRL-V rather than dealing with all those mouse clicks. If you take a moment to look up a keyboard shortcut whenever you find yourself doing the same task more than once or twice, it'll pay off. Then you can start calling yourself a Google Sheets "Power User" for sure!

Common actions

Select column	Ctrl + Space
Select row	Shift + Space
Select all	Ctrl + a
Undo	Ctrl + z
Redo	Ctrl + y
	Ctrl + Shift + z
Find	Ctrl + f
Find and replace	Ctrl + h
Fill range	Ctrl + Enter
Fill down	Ctrl + d
Fill right	Ctrl + r
Save	Ctrl + s
(every change is saved automatically in Drive)	
Open	Ctrl + o
Print	Ctrl + p
Copy	Ctrl + c
Cut	Ctrl + x
Paste	Ctrl + v
Paste values only	Ctrl + Shift + v
Show common keyboard shortcuts	Ctrl + /
Compact controls	Ctrl + Shift + f
Input tools on/off	Ctrl + Shift + k
(available in spreadsheets in non-Latin languages)	
Select input tools	Ctrl + Alt + Shift + k
Search the menus	Alt + /

Format cells

Bold	Ctrl + b
Underline	Ctrl + u
Italic	Ctrl + i
Strikethrough	Alt + Shift + 5
Center align	Ctrl + Shift + e
Right align	Ctrl + Shift + r
Apply top border	Alt + Shift + 1
Apply right border	Alt + Shift + 2
Apply bottom border	Alt + Shift + 3
Apply left border	Alt + Shift + 4
Remove borders	Alt + Shift + 6
Apply outer border	Alt + Shift + 7
	Ctrl + Shift + 7
Insert link	Ctrl + k
Insert time	Ctrl + Shift + ;
Insert date	Ctrl + ;
Insert date and time	Ctrl + Alt + Shift + ;
Format as decimal	Ctrl + Shift + 1
Format as time	Ctrl + Shift + 2
Format as date	Ctrl + Shift + 3
Format as currency	Ctrl + Shift + 4
Format as percentage	Ctrl + Shift + 5
Format as exponent	Ctrl + Shift + 6
Clear formatting	Ctrl + \

Navigate spreadsheet

Move to first cell in row with data	Ctrl + Left arrow
Move to top left of sheet	Ctrl + Search + Left arrow
Move to last cell in row with data	Ctrl + Right arrow
Move to bottom right of sheet	Ctrl + Search + Right arrow
Scroll to active cell	Ctrl + Backspace
Display list of sheets	Alt + Shift + k
Open hyperlink	Alt + Enter
Open Explore	Alt + Shift + x
Go to side panel	Alt + Shift + . Alt + Shift + ,
Move focus out of spreadsheet	Ctrl + Alt + Shift + m
Move to quicksum *(when a range of cells is selected)*	Alt + Shift + q
Move focus to popup *(for links, bookmarks, and images)*	holding Ctrl + Alt, press e then p
Open drop-down menu on filtered cell	Ctrl + Alt + r
Open revision history	Ctrl + Alt + Shift + h
Open chat inside the spreadsheet	Shift + Esc
Close drawing editor	Ctrl + Esc Shift + Esc

Edit notes and comments

Insert/edit note	Shift + Search + 2
Insert/edit comment	Ctrl + Alt + m
Open comment discussion thread	Ctrl + Alt + Shift + a
Enter current comment	holding Ctrl + Alt, press e then c

Open a menu

File menu	Alt + f
Edit menu	Alt + e
View menu	Alt + v
Insert menu	Alt + i
Format menu	Alt + o
Data menu	Alt + d
Tools menu	Alt + t
Open insert menu	Ctrl + Alt + = (with cells selected)
Open delete menu	Ctrl + Alt + - (with cells selected)
Form menu *(present when the spreadsheet is connected to a form)*	Alt + m
Add-ons menu	Alt + n
Help menu	Alt + h
Accessibility menu *(present when screen reader support is enabled)*	Alt + a
Sheet menu *(copy, delete, and other sheet actions)*	Ctrl + Shift + s
Context menu	Ctrl + Shift + \

Add or change rows and columns

Insert rows above	Ctrl + Alt + = (with rows selected)
	Alt + i, then r
Insert rows below	Alt + i, then w
Insert columns to the left	Ctrl + Alt + = (with columns selected)
	Alt + i, then c
Insert columns to the right	Alt + i, then o
Delete rows	Ctrl + Alt + - (with rows selected)
	Alt + e, then d
Delete columns	Ctrl + Alt + - (with columns selected)
	Alt + e, then e
Hide rows	Ctrl + Alt + 9
Hide columns	Ctrl + Alt + 0
Group rows or columns	Alt + Shift + Right arrow
Ungroup rows or columns	Alt + Shift + Left arrow
Expand grouped rows or columns	Alt + Shift + Down arrow
Collapse grouped rows or columns	Alt + Shift + Up arrow

Use formulas

Show all formulas	Ctrl + ~
Insert array formula	Ctrl + Shift + Enter
Collapse an expanded array formula	Ctrl + e
Show/hide formula help	Shift + Search + 1
(when entering a formula)	

Help for screen readers

Turn on screen reader support	Ctrl + Alt + z
Learn more about using Google Sheets with a screen reader	
Read column	Ctrl + Alt + Shift + c
Read row	Ctrl + Alt + Shift + r

CAN YOU DO IT?

*A*nd there we are. We looked at all the various features, menus, topics, tips, and major add-ons that can make your switch to Google Sheets from some other spreadsheet system possible.

So the only real question now is whether or not you *can* make the switch. Google Sheets does Pivot Tables, Conditional formatting, Macros, Slicers, and most of the same features and tools offered by Excel. There are still five areas that I can think of where Sheets comes up a little short in comparison to Excel, LibreOffice, and other spreadsheets:

Visual Basic and Coding

Although there is a JavaScript editor included, it's not the same language as Excel's VBA, so that might be a sore spot for very advanced users. For most people, the toolset offered by Google is more than enough. VBA scripts *can* usually be ported to Javascript, but it's not an easy or fast job.

Google Drive Limitations

As flexible as the Google ecosystem is, there are built-in limitations. For example, sometimes a company requires the use of a very specific font. If that exact font isn't built into Google Docs/Sheets, then you cannot add it. There's usually something very close to what you're looking for, but if you need **exactly** one font, then this is a problem.

Size Limitations

I have known people who have uploaded huge Excel sheets into Sheets and then couldn't productively use them because they were too unwieldy to use in a web browser. Even though they technically worked, they were painfully slow. Whether this is a limitation of the computer's RAM, limitations in Internet speed, or a limitation of Google Sheets itself, I cannot say, but there are comes a point when files are just too large.

Printing

Although you do get a number of options for printing, the printer dialog doesn't compare with Excel. It's not *bad* exactly, but if there are advanced Excel printing features that you need, this is something to look into *before* you make the switch.

Legal Restrictions

This isn't specifically a technological limitation, but it's something to consider. Some government and corporate agencies **do not allow anything** to be stored in the cloud. Yes, Google is very safe, but it's not top-secret-government safe. You're probably already aware of the rules that apply to your job, so if this is going to be a problem for you, you already know it.

For most of us, the limitations above don't apply, so Google Sheets can do everything we need in a spreadsheet system. In addition, new features are constant being added. When I started this book, *Slicers* were not a feature yet. Halfway through writing the book, they added that feature. This is one of the benefits of cloud-based software. They don't need to wait for a yearly event or a "point release," they can just release a new feature when it's ready. Be sure to check under the help menu's "What's New" section at least once a month, as it's a *very* actively developed system.

Good luck switching!

ABOUT THE AUTHOR

I am a former College IT Instructor with an extensive background in computers dating back to the 1980s. Currently, I write on a wide array of topics from computers, to world religions, to ham radio, and I've even released an occasional short horror tale.

―――――

I'd love to hear your stories of success and failure with the iPad and getting away from the standard PC world. If there's something you would like to see in a future edition of the book, or otherwise have suggestions, please drop me a note. Contact me at:

Web: http://BrianSchell.com
Email: brian@brianschell.com

Also, please join my email update list— There's NO weekly SPAM or filler material, only announcements of new books or major updates.

Email update link: http://brianschell.com/list/

If you have a suggestion or find a mistake, email me about it, and I'll get it into an updated edition of the book. Got a gripe, complaint, question, or just adoring fan mail? Same thing!

LEAVE A REVIEW

If this book helped you, please leave a review where you purchased this book. Reviews are the best way to help out!

SHARE WITH YOUR FRIENDS

Did you enjoy this book? Please use the buttons below to spread the word to your friends and followers.

twitter.com/BrianSchell

facebook.com/Brian.Schell

instagram.com/brian_schell

pinterest.com/brianschell

ALSO BY BRIAN SCHELL

Amateur Radio

• D-Star for Beginners

• Echolink for Beginners

• DMR for Beginners Using the Tytera MD-380

• SDR for Beginners with the SDRPlay

• Programming Amateur Radios with CHIRP

• FM Satellite Communications for Beginners

• Trunking Scanners for Beginners Using the Uniden TrunkTracker

Technology

• Going Chromebook: Living in the Cloud

• Going Chromebook: Mastering Google Docs

• Computing with the Raspberry Pi: Command Line and GUI Linux (Technology in Action)

• Going Text: Mastering the Power of the Command Line

• Going iPad: Ditching the Desktop

• DOS Today: Running Vintage MS-DOS Games and Apps on a Modern Computer

Old-Time Radio Listener's Guides

• OTR Listener's Guide to Dark Fantasy

• OTR Listener's Guide to Box 13

The Five-Minute Buddhist Series

• The Five-Minute Buddhist

• The Five-Minute Buddhist Returns

• The Five-Minute Buddhist Meditates

• The Five-Minute Buddhist's Quick Start Guide to Buddhism

• Teaching and Learning in Japan: An English Teacher Abroad

Fiction with Kevin L. Knights:

• Tales to Make You Shiver

• Tales to Make You Shiver 2

• Random Acts of Cloning

• Jess and the Monsters

.

CPSIA information can be obtained
at www.ICGtesting.com
Printed in the USA
LVHW080559030520
654905LV00005B/1997